LORRAINE AND JAMES

LORRAINE AND JAMES

GLOBAL URBAN LITERATURE

VOLUME ONE ✦ ISSUE ONE

EDITOR
Jasai Madden

CONSULTING EDITOR
Daniel Jaffe

POETRY EDITOR
Britni Jackson

COPY EDITOR
Alice Peck

TYPESETTING & LAYOUT
Duane Stapp

COVER ARTWORK
Jonas Lerman

WEB DESIGNER
Jonas Lerman

PUBLISHED TRIANNUALLY (3x/yr)
in summer, fall and winter by LanguageArts Publishing.
3227 West Magnolia Blvd, Suite 406, Burbank, CA 91505-2818
Telephone: 818/256-4503
www.lorraineandjames.com

PRINTED IN U.S.A.

Subscriptions Rates: Order online (www.lorraineandjames.com) USA: One Year-$27,
Individual copies-$12, Canada: One Year-$37, Individual copies-$18,
International: One Year-$40, Individual Copies-$19.

Submissions are read year round. Please review our submissions guidelines at
www.lorraineandjames.com for further details.

CONTENTS

NON-FICTION

AN INTERVIEW WITH...

EDITOR'S NOTE

In the spring of 2004, while nursing anxious knots in my belly over my failure to get my own stories down on paper, I drove alone over the hills of Encino, California to attend a reading at the UCLA's Hammer Museum. I had never done anything as artistically indulgent as that before and was unsure of just what I would experience as a result. I imagined that there would be clusters of the television stereotypes present: thin sophisticated patron-of-the-arts women with severe buns or razor-edged bobs; quirky painters with suit jackets worn haphazard over wrinkled t-shirts and long flimsy hair brought into discipline for the occasion with a single rubber band; and Seekers— young people, men and women who dream in full storylines, their hearts beating them into a subtle madness while waiting for the day that the soft spotlight on the stage at the front of that rented space would be theirs to fill.

We were all there. Programs in hand, hushing ourselves into a prepared silence, we watched as a man, apparently Jewish, not tall, and slightly balding but with full purpose, took the stage. After situating himself behind the podium, he began in perfect cadence and with flawless inflection to tell a story about the final moments of a longstanding marriage. This story, as simple as those two characters and the single scene they inhabited, brought me to a place I had never been; made me, a young woman with none of my own similar tumult to share, privy to the weighted center of their lives. Being in their midst all at once broke my heart and sat sweetly next to my neglected writer soul.

Later that night I thanked him. In the subsequent months I took his short story class. And finally, I sought his counsel when I realized that the more stories I read, the more stories I wanted to—needed to—read. I confided in him that I was so sure that other readers who were as enraptured by great storytelling as I, must feel the same way and that I wanted to make room for more of them; more stories to be told, more intimacies to be shared, more worlds to be explored, and that I planned to do it though *Lorraine and James*.

This man, this writer, and the unmistakable voices that he found himself in concert with, made me know that words and the stories they tell when they are so meticulously woven together, are the way in which we will find ourselves shoulder to shoulder, seeing our reflection in another's eyes, easily and completely connected.

Lorraine and James exists so that everyone with a powerful, wonderful, or whimsical story gets to tell it. So that characters, neighborhoods and instances too often out of range to be found in so many publications, might be given a chance to break through and fall squarely into our notice. Our mission proclaims that we intend to act as a conduit through which a writer from anywhere will be able to connect with readers everywhere. Just you wait and see.

In the process of creating *Lorraine and James* I have learned to be grateful for art, for the people who so fearlessly create it, and for the grace that canopies their journeys. I believe that stories and all things magical like them, are simply a testament of one's firm will and unfaltering faith. For this, and you, and everything, I am indebted.

Take care and be well,

Jasai Madden
Editor-In-Chief
Lorraine and James

Say something. Do Something. Read something.

ACKNOWLEDGMENTS

There is no wind, row.

I have no idea who this quote belongs to but it is the perfect sentiment for this moment. A moment when people from far and wide—Oakland to Connecticut are holding in their hands one girls' tiny germ of a notion. A notion that was in fact so small, so vague in the beginning that even as I worked until my tired eyes met the sun, I was unprepared for the idea that this was ever anything that I could execute to completion. But the following people provided wings when there was no wind and strength to help keep this project moving when unexpected turns were taken and many moves were executed in the deepest, densest dark. Having each of these individuals involved in this project whether it was in thought or in deed helped me realize that all I really needed was solid interest, honest passion and constant dedication and it could all be done.

Thank you to the following people in no particular order for believing in dreams and words and me: Dan Jaffe, Stacey Anderson, Kymberle Gamel-Jenkins, Juanita Payne, Jennifer Yester, Belinda Johnson, Curry Michels, Nicholas Montemarano, LaTosha French, Dee Stewart, Felicia Pride, every writer who submitted work to *Lorraine and James*, Britni Jackson, Margo Slucter, Janay Chapin. And to my great gifts on the planet Brooklyn; Alice Peck and Duane Stapp you are the best kind of strangers; friends in waiting. Your work is impeccable and priceless. Jonas you are a young man with great gifts and a prodigy's vision.

Thank you for you patience and tireless work. Caleb, you are my first partner, my muse, my son. And to Alexander, you are so much of why I did not fail.

Acknowledgments

This first issue of *Lorraine and James* is dedicated to three women who walked in front of me so that now I could stand and not falter and one little woman whose shoes are tiny enough still, to move audaciously through her days in my shadow. For Elizabeth, Gertrude, Julia and Stori.

SWEET POTATO AND COCONUT

Pamela MacIsaac

McGregor stared out the window, index finger frozen above *J*, arrested in full flight, an idea spinning away from him as he watched an object—a small piece of wood, a rock, a penny—fly past his daughter's head. Eva's delicate six-year-old neck was bent over an intricate game, intense and solitary above a paper and straw flag stuck into a scant hill of cindery gray city earth scraped up from the cement floor of McGregor's poor excuse for a front deck. He'd needed some peace, disguised it as a half hour of pretend work, and had sent her out front with a stern injunction to remain within the perimeter of the deck. He could see her easily from where he sat and periodically shifted his eyes from the computer screen to her small form, calm now, concentrating on her private game instead of hurtling around his cramped living room.

He relaxed, allowed himself to slump in his chair, shift his butt back into the seat instead of perching on the edge ready to chase Eva when she made one of her impulsive, suicidal dashes into the street or held her hand out to the neighbor's nervous, child-hating dog. Maybe he needed to trust Eva more, he thought; give her more responsibility for keeping safe. Other kids played outside alone, right? He'd seen them, roaming the neighborhood at all hours of the day or night, unaccompanied by adults, raising hell on their scooters and bikes; shocking to McGregor, used to the carefully shepherded routines of his nieces and nephews, his own child.

As he watched, another missile grazed the end of Eva's thick brown pony-tail and hit the cement with a metallic clang; a penny that time, definitely a penny McGregor thought, copper glinting in the sun as the coin tumbled to a stop by the railing. Eva's head swiveled, her attention broken by the impact of the coin. She gazed upward with a questioning expression then looked through the window at McGregor. He saw her mouth moving. "What was that, Dad?" He jumped out of his seat, chair legs squeaking, scarring even further the heavily grooved wooden floor.

McGregor ran through his living room. Two large steps and he was at his front door, stumbling slightly over Eva's discarded sneakers and sandals, her Hello Kitty purse. "Goddamn it, Eva!" he growled through gritted teeth, wondering why the child had to bring so many pairs of shoes, articles of clothing, books, and toys to his small apartment each weekend, introducing chaos into his meticulously arranged clutter. On one occasion she brought an old manual typewriter, claiming *she* had work to do too, and on another occasion, a gerbil belonging to a neighbor and entrusted to her care for the weekend. McGregor could always see the amusement in his ex-wife's eyes, hated her small smile, her satisfaction at his poorly concealed irritation as Eva hauled more junk out of the trunk of their—Sarah's—old Honda.

In the communal hallway, he closed his nose against the funk of cigarettes and well-used bedding, a smell he had come to hate, passionately. It was, to him, the odor of failure. He burned incense in his own apartment, plugged the bottom of the door with wet towels, anything to stop the miasma of poverty from seeping into his furniture, his clothes, his hair, his life. He'd rented this apartment because it was close to his—Sarah's—house and was the cheapest he could find in the neighborhood. Regret of various kinds swamped every time he came in or out.

Stepping through the front door, McGregor craned his neck to look at the balcony of the apartment above him. He could see a pair of chubby brown legs hanging through gaps in the iron rail. McGregor walked further out onto his deck and leaned against his own railing. A small face, framed by two fists on rusted wrought iron stared down at him. As McGregor watched, a bright pink tongue protruded from the face and waved at him.

"Uh, hi up there!" McGregor heard his own voice, dismayingly, falsely jocular, the tone of a person uncomfortable with other people's children. "You shouldn't throw stuff you know. It could hurt someone."

"Yeah!" cried Eva. "You could hurt *me!*"

"Hello!" the child sang. "Hello, hello, *hellooooo!*"

McGregor blinked. "Did you hear what I said?"

"What you say?"

"I said you can't throw things from up there. It's dangerous." McGregor paused and waited for a sign of comprehension. The child grinned at him, gap-toothed, unapologetic. *"La la la la la!"* he sang. McGregor gave up. "Is your mom there?"

"Mommy?" The little boy shook his head and started to laugh.

"Do you speak English?" Eva said suddenly in a loud, strangely adult voice, reminding McGregor eerily of Sarah.

"Eva!" McGregor shook his head at her. Eva shrugged.

"Eva!" The boy called, echoing McGregor. "Eva!"

McGregor remembered hearing the tail end of a story, gossip among his neighbors, the situation of the family upstairs from him, two boys and a grandmother he now recalled. "Is your grandma around? Can you ask her to come out?"

The boy stood up, shirt falling loose. McGregor was shocked to see the tops of the child's bare legs, his genitals. Beside him, Eva gasped, "Daddy!" she whispered, horrified and pleased, "that little boy isn't wearing any pants!"

"I can see that, Eva." McGregor shushed her with his hand, and then beckoned. Eva stood up, brushed down her green pedal pushers, and walked over to put her head against McGregor's thin hip. He put his hand on the top of her head and felt the warmth from the sun seep into his palm. "You should have a…"

McGregor's head reared back, his hands flew up automatically to guard his face as a sharp pain struck him above the right eyebrow. The impact blinded him temporarily. He opened his eye to see a refracted light in the center of his field of vision, sunlight broken into prisms by the pain. Somewhere above his vibrating head there was terrified laughter, whoops of triumph. "God*damn* it!" McGregor cried.

"Daddy!" Eva began to jump up and down and point, tears in her eyes. "You're bleeding! Daddy, you're bleeding!" McGregor brought his hand away and looked at the blood, felt it dripping through his eyebrow. He felt a tearing rage, the urge to scream. He struggled to keep himself calm.

"Okay, Eva. Okay. Just calm down. Get daddy a chair, will you?"

Eva began to cry hysterically. "Eva! Please! Get me a chair." The child gulped down her sobs. She jumped from foot to foot then began to drag one of McGregor's old lawn chairs over to where he stood, sagging against the rail. McGregor lowered himself into the lawn chair and pressed his palm harder against his forehead.

"Get me a towel, Eva. And *stop crying! Please!*" Eva's ebbing but still audible sobs mixed with the wild laughter from above. His daughter's dancing panic made McGregor's heart flutter, made him unable to think. When she dashed into the house, he tried to collect himself. The boy on the balcony above ventured back to the rail and began to call out, mockingly, "Eva! Eva! Eva! Get me a towel, Eva! Stop crying, Eva!"

McGregor, overcome with fury, leaned back in his chair and shook his fist at the child. "Shut the hell up! You hurt me, you little brat!" He felt satisfaction and shame after screaming at the child. His heart began to slow, and the beginnings of a sensible plan formed in his head. When Eva returned with a towel from the bathroom, he pressed it to his head and sighed. He reached out and took the child's trembling chin in his fingers.

"Okay, Eva. I'm going to get you to call Mommy, okay? I think she better come get you."

"Okay." Eva agreed, too quickly. "Should I call her now?"

"Yeah, I think so, sweetie." McGregor opened his eyes to look at the child. She wiped the back of her hand across her cheeks and sniffed loudly, but her chin and lips had stopped shaking. "Do you mind, much?"

"No, that's okay, Daddy." Eva's voice held pure relief. McGregor heaved himself out of the lawn chair. Resting one arm on Eva's head for support, he made slow progress into his apartment, where he collapsed on his old sofa. Eva took two skipping steps to the telephone.

"Mommy? It's me. I have to come home early. Something's happened to Daddy." The child paused. "Something hit him in the head. A rock, I think. A kid threw it." Eva held the telephone away from her ear, and spoke to McGregor. "Are you okay, Dad? Mommy wants to know." McGregor nodded, painfully.

"He's okay, I think." Eva spoke to her mother again. "Sure. See you soon." She hung up the telephone. "She's coming to get me now."

"Great, honey. Listen, I'm sorry."

"It's not your fault, Daddy. And I'll see you next week." Eva began hurriedly to pick up her belongings in the living room, made her way into the spare bedroom to pack her suitcase. McGregor, lying on the sofa, was buffeted by a wave of sorrow.

Eva emerged from the bedroom, a pair of socks in her hand. She went to the window and stood on her toes to look out over the porch rail. "She should be here any minute," she said, craning her neck, "She was having breakfast with Neil, but she said it could wait."

McGregor sat up, a hammer blow of pain in his cranium. "Neil?"

"Yeah, from the college."

"Neil, from the college?"

"He has a car you can unlock with the key chain! You just press a button." Eva turned to look at her father. "He's a dean."

McGregor tried to collect himself, quell his alarm. Don't question her, he warned himself. "Does he eat breakfast at your house often?"

"No, not really."

"No or not really, Eva? Which is it?"

"Not really, I guess. Sometimes."

"Does he sleep there the night before?"

"Daddy!" Eva laughed. "Why would he do that?"

A car honked outside the window. Eva grabbed her bag, and shoved her feet into her sneakers. "It's Mom! Bye Dad!"

McGregor stood up, conquered dizziness. "I'll come with you. I want to talk to mommy." Eva looked worried.

"Why?"

"Just some grown-up stuff." McGregor followed his daughter onto the porch, looking up to check for the boy as he passed underneath the upstairs balcony. The child could not be seen. Eva ran to her mother's car, and jumped in the passenger's side. McGregor walked around to the driver's side. As he came around the back of the car, his ex-wife rolled down her window and leaned her head out. Several dark brown curls tumbled out, contrasting with the dull tan exterior of their—her—car. She looked concerned. "Are you okay? What happened?"

"It's a long story involving an insane child, a rock, and a balcony."

"*Ow!*" Sarah squinted up at his head. "I can't see you that well. Is it bad?"

"I'll live. Who's Neil?"

Sarah ignored the question, pretended it had not been asked, a longstanding, frustrating ability. She pulled her head back into the car, addressed the steering wheel. "You should go to Emergency, Wayne. That might need stitches."

"I'll be fine. I asked you a question, Sarah. Who's Neil?"

Sarah lifted her hands to the steering wheel and stared at them. McGregor felt a familiar rush of anger at her obstinacy. "I think it's a fair question."

"I don't." Sarah rolled up her window, and started the car with a roar. McGregor stepped back into the street, heard a honk as a driver swerved to miss him. Sarah pulled away with a wrench of the wheel, and Eva turned to wave. McGregor moved to the sidewalk and watched until the car, *his* car, turned the corner. Reaching up, he grabbed a handful of leaves from the tree above him, ripped them violently from the branch.

Inside his apartment, he sifted through his nearly empty freezer, found a forgotten bag of peas, and carried these to the sofa, tossing them back and forth to relieve the cold ache in his palms. He sat down and tried to remove the towel and found it had stuck fast to his cut, glued in place with partially coagulated blood. Slowly he peeled the towel off, groaning as the cut reopened. He applied the bag of peas and felt the blood begin to seep underneath, slipped his legs over the front of the sofa, and stretched out on his back, legs prickled by sweat and the harsh little nubs of the upholstery. Sitting up again, he swung his legs to the ground and stood up slowly, wincing at the lightning forks of pain.

A search for band aids, for gauze and tape, anything to staunch the maddening trickle of his own blood, protect his vulnerable skull from the foul air of his apartment, make him feel as though he'd actually *done* something, taken some action to repair himself, reseal his outsides. Still holding the bloodied bag of peas to his head, he rifled through the medicine cabinet, accidentally pushing toothpaste, a jar of cream, and his razor into the sink. They rattled against the porcelain, loud as gunfire. Underneath a bottle of eye drops, McGregor found three band-aids, laid flat against the glass shelf. The paper on the bottom one was greasy, and the top one was shriveled with dampness and old age, but the middle band-aid appeared to be relatively clean and usable. McGregor lowered his bag of peas to the edge of the sink, and began to unwrap the band-aid, cursing as it slipped from his shaking fingers, eventually managing to extract it from the paper.

Leaning in to the mirror, he examined his gory forehead, surprised at the small size of the cut. "Scalp wounds bleed heavily," he reminded himself. He placed the band-aid carefully on the back of the toilet and washed his face with cold water. The water stung his forehead, revealed skin of a strange, yellowy-brown color, the precursor to a wicked purple and blue bruise, he assumed. Hands steadier, breathing deeply, he held the edges of the cut together—*Shit!*—and secured his work with the band-aid.

Exhausted now, McGregor retrieved his bag of peas, which had started to slosh unpleasantly, and resumed his prone position on the sofa. He felt his eyes begin to close. He drifted in and out of sleep, believing for long moments of half-consciousness that Sarah was there—in the kitchen cooking, upstairs at the computer, talking softly to Eva in bed. McGregor jerked awake.

He remembered a very early morning, two years ago, when he'd watched Eva and Sarah sleep, both of them on their backs, wild hair loose across white pillows. Their sleeping arrangements had become jumbled, confused; Eva in her own bed with Sarah, McGregor in the big bed with Eva, McGregor alone in Eva's bed, as he'd been the night before. Somehow, imperceptibly and by degrees, he and Sarah had stopped sleeping in the same bed, had stopped touching each other. Watching the two of them sleep, listening to Sarah snore lightly through her small nose, he'd acknowledged her relentless campaign to distance herself, her unwavering resolve to get rid of him, reckoned up the long months of near silence, the periodic bouts of ferocious criticism. She woke up and stared at him in the half-dark.

"What are you doing?" She'd whispered harshly, trying to keep from waking Eva.

McGregor considered. What was he doing, exactly, and why did he feel like a voyeur, a goddamn Peeping Tom, watching his own wife sleep? He'd sighed, dramatically and luxuriously. "I'm pretending I can keep you."

He thought about that now, the bathos of his statement met by more of Sarah's silence, his feeble attempt to wring humor out of the sad fact that he had no means of keeping her, had known from the start that she would leave him someday, move on to something, someone better, bigger and stronger. A man. He imagined Neil, Sarah's breakfast partner, picturing him as the cover of a magazine, both substantial and polished, his shoulders easily twice as wide as McGregor's own and covered in a finely woven shirt, his hand reaching to stroke Sarah's thick, tumbling hair...

Heavy, running footsteps thudded the ceiling. A door banged. Seconds later, a rhythmic thumping began, someone, the evil boy, throwing a ball against the wall, McGregor hypothesized, and catching it on the bounce. The noise ricocheted inside McGregor's aching head, swelled membranes, sent his pulse flying, and got his blood pumping. He could hear it whistling and hissing through his veins and arteries, could swear that more pumped out of his wound, an extra gush into the inadequate band-aid, down the side of his face, into his eyes and ear. McGregor roared, threw the bag of peas across the room. It hit the wall with an icy smash and slid to the floor, left a smear of blood on the wall beside his desk.

McGregor stared at the blood, jumped to his feet, and strode the short distance to his door, opening it with a swing. He hit the stairs at a run, letting his feet slam into each uncarpeted, noisy board with a satisfying jolt. Thundering thus, he became a much larger man, thigh muscles spreading, calves swelling as he stretched to meet each step. On the next landing, he raised his fist and brought it down as hard as he could on the flimsy door of the apartment above his. He waited for a few seconds, and then slammed his fist again and again, felt the door rattle in its frame, seemingly on the verge of splintering.

"Hold on. Hold on." A woman's voice came from the apartment, along with a shuffling sound, slippers on the wood floor. McGregor waited, trembling, teeth knocking with anger. "Who's there?"

"It's Wayne McGregor."

"Who?"

"Your neighbor! Your downstairs neighbor!"

"Well, what you want?"

"I want you to open the door. I want to talk to you about something."

There was quiet on the other side of the door.

"Can you open the door please?"

Nothing. McGregor banged again. He heard the woman jump on the other side of the door.

"I'm not opening the door for nobody who bangs like that."

"Your son hurt me! He threw something from your balcony and hurt me."

"He's not my son."

"Well, whoever he is, he threw a rock or something and it hit my head. My six-year-old daughter was out there, and he could have hit her. It could have killed her!" McGregor pictured Eva, crumpled on the filthy cement of the porch floor, head bloodied like his own, brain rattled, a brief, self-indulgent vision that fired his rage, stoked him, as though the child really had been injured. He pounded again, this time with both fists.

"I'm callin' the landlord! I'm callin' the police!" the woman shouted from the other side. McGregor heard the rock-throwing child begin to wail in the background.

McGregor took a step back into the hallway. He listened to himself breathing, tried to smooth his ragged intake, puffing exhale, pulling in air through his nostrils, releasing it through his lips. The woman's invocation of authority, the child's crying, played to his middle-class fears and quelled him. He hated his apartment, hated this building, but did not want to be evicted, like a criminal, a miscreant, a drunken undergraduate, or a drug dealer. Breathing more easily, he descended the stairs, careful to walk quietly and despising himself for it. In his apartment, he returned to the sofa, lay stiff, listening to the silence upstairs, replaying his own behavior again and again, his knuckles then the side meat of his fisted hand, the woman's frightened voice, the child. He wondered, who of the other tenants had overheard his shouting? Which ones would shake their heads, clucking at the scene? Which ones would sympathize with him, with what he'd endured?

A knock at the door, a brisk hand, brought him to his feet. "Shit," he said under his breath, thinking police, a delegation of outraged tenants, a burly son or brother seeking revenge. McGregor cowered, head bowed, fear flooding his veins, knowing he was about to pay the cost of his inappropriate acts, his threatening hands, frightening women and children.

"Mr. McGregor?" It was the woman from upstairs. "Are you in there?"

McGregor forced himself to walk the short distance across his living room and open the door. He saw a small dark brown woman, hair covered by a bright red turban, eyes veiled by large, black-framed glasses, body shrouded in a loose flowered dress. The small boy from the balcony was beside her, quiet now, fully dressed in t-shirt and jeans. The child held a bowl, covered in foil wrap.

"Mr. McGregor, Joseph here has something he wants to say." The woman bore down on the back of the child's neck with her hand, pushed the child gently forward. He hung back, pressing against her hand. She nodded down at him, then at McGregor.

"I'm sorry." The child spoke in a whisper.

McGregor waved his hands, somewhat frantically. "Oh, you know, that's alright. I mean, *I'm* sorry. I'm sorry I pounded on your door like that. It's been a bit of a tough day."

"We're real sorry you got your head hurt. It's not going to happen again. Is it, Joseph?" The child shook his head, and then smiled up at McGregor, two deep dimples flickering in his cheeks. McGregor could see the child's eyes rolling and shifting under his lowered lids, sensed the suppressed jiggle and squirm of the small body.

McGregor recovered himself. "Well, okay. Sure. We'll let it go."

"These are for you. They're pound cakes, special ones I made this morning."

"Oh no, that's not necessary."

"Yes it is. Joseph, give the man a cake." The child thrust the bowl at McGregor who lifted it, raising a buttery scent. McGregor's mouth watered; he realized he had not eaten since early that morning. Unable to wait, he ripped the foil off the top of the bowl and removed one of the thick slices, bit into the sugary crust of it, the rich orange warmth. The woman smiled.

"Sweet potatoes and coconut," she offered. "That's my secret."

McGregor held out the bowl to the woman who refused to take any, and to Joseph, who helped himself to a large one. Standing in the hallway, Joseph and McGregor ate all of the small cakes, passing the bowl back and forth between them.

FOR (*INSERT YOUR NAME HERE*),
I DID KNOW YOU

Patricia Gomes

Patricia Gomes

Where I come from
the men are rough,
the women rougher still.
Poverty breeds
weak men, unemployment being the quickest method of castration
and so, men become minute dalliances to us—
entertainment
during periods when there is no TV
or lights to read a book by when the sun goes down,
the power company not being the most charitable of institutions.

And I did not commit their names
to my Fond Recollections Box,
but neither was I ashamed,
and was only embarrassed by one
of the choices I made.

It wasn't that he was particularly ugly,
or uncouth,
or dull (most of them are, you know),
but rather just *beige.*
Everything about him colorless,
common, muted.

It was an affair that should have run its course
in two weeks, but dragged on horribly for sixteen.
He clung—like white cat hairs on your best black blazer.
And later, when I saw him on the streets,
I would cross hurriedly, turning the corner as fast as I could.
Never would I boast
(or even admit)
to my friends that I had laid with such a two-dimensional dullard.

With middle-age comes guilt,
and now rather than battle
nighttime demons that block his name from memory, I write this poem
in apology and penance,
immortalizing an ordinary man that once took the edge
off a bad summer.

A TREATISE ON THE POWER OF READING

Mark Budman (signature)

Mark Budman

like to read. When I was eight, my mother would shove me down the stairs into the cellar and throw a Dylan Thomas book at me. "Do not go gentle into that good night."

That's how I came to hate poetry. It always smelled musty. But I like to read everything else.

My friend Bill complained I never return the books I borrow. But how can I? I devour them. I savor them. One word between heartbeats, one sentence between eye blinks.

I like to read. When I was seven, my mother gave me *The Brothers Grimm Tales* for my birthday. She had quit reading to me by then. I would sit in the closet on a pile of dirty underwear, with a flashlight, reading, trying not to listen to her making out with men in the bed we shared.

In court, my former wife complained that I spent all I made on books. That was a lie. I bought bookshelves and humidity controllers too. I don't want my books to get ruined.

I like to read. When I was six, my mother would read to me from Dr. Seuss. She was often drunk, and I buried my face in her sweater.

At night, I dream of termites burrowing through my books, killing me.

I like to read. When I was five, my mom and I colored a picture book. My father had just left us, and she kissed me often. I would ask her about the tears in her eyes, and she'd say that a bee stung her.

My neighbors probably think I do drugs because I so rarely leave the house.

I like to read. When I was four, my daddy and mommy read me nursery rhymes in my bedroom. I would fall asleep while they would look at me, grinning. I wish I had a child I could read to.

I like to read. I would bequeath all my books to Bill, but he died last year, two days shy of his fiftieth birthday. So I will bequeath them to the local library. I imagine kids taking a break from reading, chatting, asking each other, "Did you hear about the guy who shot himself in the book store? Was he a weirdo or what?" And I wouldn't be there to tell them that the right word is *eccentric*.

BLOOD OF THE LAMB

Jess Stuart

Jess Stuart

Mother is knitting again. Every spare minute. Needles clicking in a white-hot fury. It's been only a few months, but already she's done so much, made so many impossibly small garments, the size to break your heart imagining the tiny feet, the bitty arms that will fill them. She hides her work if she hears Ab padding around. So far, this has been our little secret, hers and mine, but today might be the telling day, who can say?

She smiles when she sees me. Her fingers never stop moving.

"Look!" I say turning profile and pulling my robe tight from the back. "I've swallowed the moon!" Proudly I massage the delicate rise in my middle.

Mother laughs and shakes her head.

"Plenty of time yet," she tells me.

Click, click, clickity-click.

She knits so quickly blue sparks fly off the ends of her needles.

"What is it this time?" I ask, fingering the knobbly fabric unfurling between her palms like a sacred scroll.

"A blanket for the little one."

Click, click, clickity-click.

"But red?" I say with a pretend frown. "Aren't you afraid you'll give her nightmares?"

She flashes me a withering look and continues her work. It's a familiar game between us, a sisterly tease, womanly mischief.

I ease myself down by her feet, rest my head against her knee, and watch my mother create comfort and warmth, stitch by stitch, row upon row. At the same time, I think I can hear the baby being knit together inside my womb, bone by bone, joint upon joint, click, click, clickity-click.

Em smiles as I watch her work.

"When are *you* going to learn to use the needles?" she asks.

I laugh and shake my head.

"Plenty of time yet," I tell her.

Just then, I feel a quickening beneath my heart like the fluttering pulse-beat in a lover's throat—my child, dwelling between the now and the not yet, making her presence known.

I kneel up and clasp my hands over Em's knees as I did when I was little and she would hear my prayers. The blanket grows down over my hands, my arms.

"I have a confession," I whisper.

Her head tilts towards me, dark eyes dancing.

"At night," I say, "when the simoom sweeps across the sill all warm-blooded and womanly, and silence stops up my ears to all but the sound of my own heart, I roll to my back, dip my fingers in lamp oil and anoint this little newcomer bobbing so contentedly between my hips."

"Hm," she murmurs. "I wondered why all my oil was disappearing."

Click, click, clickity-click.

"I slide my fingers over brown, round flesh until I feel her little head and two tiny hands, sharp as stars, pressing against my skin, so eager for the blessing! Then I listen while she sings her psalms and chants her canticles, trilling away in the tongues of angels and men. And do you know, she sways as she prays, back and forth, back and forth, just as the rabbis do!"

"Devout little Jewess, isn't she?" Em pauses a moment to count stitches. "Thought of any names yet?"

I nod. "Tikkun Olam."

Em's fingers hesitate. "The Mending of the World?" she asks.

I nod again.

Her eyes look past me towards some future time. Then, "She'll get 'Tik,' you know."

I shrug.

Silently she repeats the name to herself, gentling her lips to taste it. At last she smiles and sets her needles jabbing at each other again.

"It was the same when I carried you," she tells me. "I thought I was going to be the mother of the universe, the mother of all blessing!"

We both laugh. Then she leans forward and touches my cheek with the backs of her fingers.

"And see here," she murmurs softly, "I was! I was!"

And I love her so much, this woman, this other daughter, this mother of all blessing! I love her and I love her and I love her!

"Tell me a story," she says suddenly, forgetting who is the mother and who the daughter.

"What story do you want to hear?" I ask, pretending to pick lint off the little blanket.

"There is only one story," she says.

"Oh *that* one!" I roll my eyes. "You've heard *that* one a thousand times! Surely you don't want to hear it again!"

She pulls her lips tight and lifts an eyebrow.

"Indulge me," she says. "It's a good story. Good stories bear repeating."

"Oh alright!" I say with magnificent condescension, and settle myself once more at her feet.

"This is the story of how Lord God Elohim got himself a child by a woman of flesh."

"That's the story!" Em says, nodding with satisfaction.

And the little one within me begins to dance. She loves to hear the story as much as her *nona*.

"Well then," I begin. "One day, not so very long ago, a woman, we'll call her Ahabah..."

"Ahabah," echoes Em, "the Beloved."

"Yes, the Beloved. Well, one day, Ahabah received a visitor from the celestial courts, an emissary from Lord Elohim.

"'Shalom Ahabah!' he greeted her. "Thou art highly favored! The Lord is with thee! Blessed art thou among women!' Ahabah was perplexed and a bit unsettled..."

"As who wouldn't be to find their kitchen infested with angels?" puts in Em.

"Even so. But the angel told her not to fear, that she had been chosen to bear the Messiah!"

"Oh yes, nothing frightening about that!"

"Em, please! When Ahabah heard the angel's words, she asked quickly, 'Is it to be a boy or a girl?'

"'A boy, naturally,' the emissary sniffed. 'This child is destined to be King of All, Lord of Heaven and Earth! Of what possible good would a girl-child be?'"

I choke on my anger and turn my head away. Em gently takes my chin in her hand and looks in my eyes.

"A girl-child can be very good," she whispers, "very, *very* good!"

She nods emphatically and returns to her knitting. I follow her example, and pick up the threads of my story.

"Well, Ahabah curled her lip at the angel, but behind her hand, for her mother raised her to be polite always!"

Em chuckles softly.

"Ahabah said to the angel, 'I assume Elohim plans to consecrate one of my sons sometime after I'm married?'

"'No indeed!' The angel looked surprised. 'Lord Elohim (blessed be he!) wishes to put you with child within the hour!'

"'*What?*' Ahabah gasped. 'You mean I would become pregnant now, today? And just how would I explain such a pregnancy? I, the unmarried daughter of a priest?'

"The angel shrugged, unconcerned. 'You will have done nothing wrong,' he said. 'Why not just tell the truth?'

"'And who would believe...?' Ahabah started. 'Can't you convince God to wait until I'm married, so I might protect myself, my family, and my child from the scandal of this...blessed event?'

"The angel shook his head. 'However,' he said, 'you can take comfort knowing the token of your virginity will remain intact before, during, and after the birth of God's son. You shall be,' the angel coughed delicately into his hand, 'a *virgin* mother.'

"'A virgin mother,' repeated Ahabah contemptuously. "I'll be sure to explain *that* to the crowd as they're stoning me to death!'

"The angel appeared unmoved. 'Only an unmarried woman will suit. Elohim (blessed be he!) desires his...mistress...to be a dove undefiled, a garden enclosed, a fountain sealed, a...'

"'A virgin,' Ahabah finished flatly.

"'Even so.'"

I look up at Em. "I don't understand why Ahabah had to be a virgin."

She stops knitting for a moment and looks up to the rafters. "Hymens," she answers at last, "are *very* important to men! *They* say that if a woman's hymen is intact, then she is pure—as if a woman's purity could be tied to a little tag of flesh! *I* think they insist on a hymen in their brides because then there's no pressure on them to be decent lovers! 'What does it matter how poorly I treat her?' they tell themselves. 'She won't know any better!' Em shakes her head ruefully. "No doubt it was the same with Elohim. This was his first time too, you know, and if he had tried to approach an experienced woman, the inevitable comparisons would likely have made him too nervous to...well..." She gestures with a decidedly limp hand and snickers before returning to her knitting.

"*Em!*" I pretend to be shocked.

She shrugs, smiles, and continues knitting.

"At any rate," I go on, "the angel tried to convince Ahabah how privileged she should feel, 'From the creation of the first life-giver, Eve, Elohim (blessed be he!) has wished to mate with your kind. Through the ages, he's watched you all, spying from the bushes while you bathe, peeking under the covers while you sleep. He was the invisible voyeur at every marriage bed, the envious spectator peeping down from the shadowy corners of every brothel. Now he desires a woman of his own, someone on whom he can inscribe his very image in the form of his only begotten son. But not just any woman will do! Elohim (blessed be he!) has set his heart on you Ahabah, and comes to you humbly, asking that you accept his proposal.'

"Ahabah paced the kitchen and thought, *Elohim wishes to satisfy his almighty lust on me and breed me. And as a reward, he will leave me, what? A daughter to comfort me? No! But a son to raise alone, in poverty and shame, a son who will someday leave me to be about his father's business.*

"The angel followed her with his eyes. 'You understand what's being offered here?' he asked.

"'I believe I do,' Ahabah replied. 'The only question seems to be, do I wish to be God's whore and his breeding cow?'

"The emissary considered this for a moment. 'Well, do you?'

"And what did Ahabah say to that?" Em asks, as if she doesn't already know.

"Ahabah, the Beloved, said nothing, but seized her mother's broom, and swept that angel-pimp right out the door!"

Em cackles delightedly. "Swept him out the door! Ha! Took her em's broom and gave him the brush-off! Made a clean sweep! Oh, such a daughter! Such a woman!" She takes a moment to control herself, then asks, "But wasn't Ahabah afraid Elohim would select a more…compliant candidate?"

"That's *exactly* what Ahabah was hoping! Then there would be no problem, and she could live her life in peace!" I sigh. "But such was not to be. For Elohim…"

"Blessed be he!"

"Blessed be he! Our Lord God Elohim, the Great Smiter, was himself smitten. Ahabah heard him sniffing around the back door and whimpering under her windowsill at night like a puppy left out in the rain.

"'Open to me, my sister, my love, my dove, my undefiled!'

"On and on, all night, every night.

"'Oh, shut up and go away!' Ahabah would shout from her bed."

Em lifts an amused eyebrow. "You know," she says, trying to be serious, "Moses took off his sandals when he heard the voice of God."

"As did Ahabah!" I assure her. "Took off her sandals and flung them right out the window at God's head! At last he got the message and left, but she could still hear him night after night, howling his frustration at the desert moon."

"Poor Elohim!" Em giggles. "Poor King of the Universe!"

She waits for me to continue, and when I don't, she urges impatiently, "Well? What finally happened between Ahabah and Elohim?"

"Ah well, when Ahabah realized that Elohim's panting lust for her was making him stupid, a superbly wicked idea occurred to her! So one night, like Ruth, she bathed and anointed herself..."

"With lamp oil?"

"Hush Em! She put on her best clothes and set about finding a thrashing place."

"You mean *threshing* place, don't you?" Em interrupts. "Like in Ruth's story? *Threshing* place?"

I look at her steadily. "Ruth threshed. Ahabah was looking to *thrash*."

"Oh!" she says as understanding dawns. "Oh-ho!"

Click, click, clickity-click!

"Ahabah scented God's passion in the wilderness, followed him through the badlands, overtook him in the desert and seduced him in the sand! 'I have come to give you my love,' she told him, dropping her robe.

Elohim gasped as he gazed on her, and flowers burst into bloom, water began flowing uphill, and a single, perfect snowflake fluttered to the sand! Mighty Elohim fell to his knees, clasped his beloved around her waist, and yipped like a wounded jackal! He wept so many tears, all the desert wadis overflowed their banks!

Then he kissed her, kissed her with the kisses of his mouth, drinking deeply the milk and honey beneath her tongue, the spiced wine from the chalice of her navel. Scrambling up the stately palm tree of her body, he laid hold the glorious clusters of her breasts. His left hand was under her head, and his right hand, his fine right hand, his excellent right hand, his remarkably nimble right hand ca-*ressed* her!"

"Ah!" breathes Em, eyes closed, knitting momentarily suspended. "How knowledgeable he was for his first time! Ahabah was blessed to have so skillful a lover!"

"Well, he was God after all!" I remind her. "And then, at precisely the moment he was about to part her jewel-like thighs, Ahabah stopped him. 'Just one more thing,' she said.

"Elohim gnashed his teeth. '*What?!*'

"'We will love until I'm pregnant,' she insisted.

"'Yes, yes, of course!'

"'With a *girl*-child!'"

"And what did Elohim say to that?" Em asks, as she always does at this point in the story.

"He said, 'Anything! Anything!'" and I flap my hands frantically back and forth, mimicking his infinite agitation.

Em bends double with laughter. "Anything! Anything!" she hoots, repeating both word and gesture. "Jezebel! Delilah!" She wipes her eyes on her sleeve. "Elohim would have promised her half of heaven to get between her legs!"

We laugh together.

"Then Ahabah warned him, 'Remember,' she said, 'you have given your word! A god who breaks their word ceases to be god!'"

"What then?" Em asks.

"He said, '*Chanan.*' Just that, and so quietly, at first Ahabah wasn't sure he'd spoken at all."

A pitying look softens Em's dark eyes. "'*Chanan,*'" she whispers. "'Mercy.' He begged for mercy. Poor thing! Poor little god! I hope she didn't keep him waiting long after that!"

"Ah no," I say dreamily, picturing the scene. "There was no waiting after that! From a long way off you could see the mighty cloud of dust rising above the place where they wrestled in the sand. All night they twined, twisted, wriggled and slithered together, a couple of frenzied serpents loosed from Eden, each tempting the other to fall and rise again. Lips and fingers sticky with the juice of forbidden fruit, they were naked and unashamed. He was to her a pillar of fire. And she was to him a crown of thorns wound tight about his heart. The virgin woman, the virgin god. Fire and ice, thunder and silence, wanting, having, and letting go. And now..."

"And now, a child!" Em reaches over and gleefully pats my belly. "Our Messiah-baby, my granddaughter, Tikkun Olam! Oh, the stories I'll tell her! The songs I'll sing to her!" She touches my face again and says, "All generations will call you blessed!"

And we lose ourselves in this moment of grace, until a small noise from the doorway wrenches it away. Ab is standing there, head bowed, one hand on the door jamb, the other over his face. He is weeping.

"Abba!" I cry, rushing to him. He lets me guide him to a chair, then buries his face in his hands and moans as if in pain. Out of the corner of my eye I see Tik's little red blanket trembling on Em's needles.

"Ab," I say, trying to soothe, "Ab, I am growing a wonder inside my body! God and I, we..."

"I was standing in the doorway a long time," he mutters between his fingers. "I heard the story."

"Then why do you weep?" I touch his tortured face, trying to see myself in his eyes.

"This is *God's* child," I tell him, "his daughter! Who knows what she'll do? Feed the multitude, heal the sick, maybe even raise the dead!"

"And who would notice?!" Ab shouts, roughly brushing away my hands from his face. "Who would even notice? Tell me that!"

I glance at Em in confusion. But her gaze is lowered, her fingers still.

"Abba, I don't underst—"

"So a woman comes into the world and feeds the multitude. What's so unusual about that? Women turn stones into bread every day! Women already heal the sick, and they do better than raise the dead—they bring forth new life! Women? *They save the world every day!* If the Messiah comes as a woman..." he shakes his head. "What ridiculous redundancy!"

Em gently pulls on the loose end of the blanket with just enough firmness to begin unravelling it.

"Abba," I say, "please! There's so much God's daughter could teach us!"

"And who will listen to her? Other women? Don't you understand? Women don't need the Messiah! Men do! If the Messiah comes as a woman, do you think anything she says will ever be heard, much less written down? No, I tell you! She will be laughed to scorn! She will be silenced, shunned, ignored, forgotten! 'Another upstart woman who should have been beaten more often to teach her respect!'"

Em continues unravelling Tik's little red blanket. Her face is stone.

"But Ab," my voice strangles in my throat, "she will l-love us..."

He sits down beside me now and takes my hand. His voice is calmer, sadder.

"Of course she will love!" he says quietly. "She's a woman, isn't she? She will love as all women do, until her heart breaks, until the last drop of blood is poured out. She will give and forgive and sacrifice herself on Love's own altar. And men will think 'Just another victim to add to the pile,' if they think anything at all."

He brings my hand to my belly and says mournfully, "A miracle, no doubt, but a misbegotten one."

Then he raises his eyes and prays, "Lord Elohim, we are your servants, and will do what must be done. But next time, we humbly beseech you, clean up your own bloody experiment!"

The last wisp of wool uncurls from Em's needles and slips soundlessly to the floor. Abba pats my hand and heaves himself to his feet. He is muttering something under his breath, and just before he steps out into the bright sunlight, I catch the words of the prayer for the dead.

Em's naked needles are quiet now, the wool heaped in a red mess at her feet. She too quits her chair and slowly comes towards me, sorrow brimming in her eyes. The little body within mine starts to writhe and struggle and a tiny voice is shrieking, "My God, my God, why?"

"Ab doesn't believe me," I say, wrapping my arms around my body.

"Trouble is, he does."

She moves closer.

"Maybe it won't be a girl after all!" I say desperately. "Maybe it's a boy, a son, yes—yes, the *son* of God!"

"It's a girl," Em says softly and gently pulls my arm away from my belly. One by one she coaxes open my fingers, then presses her knitting needles against my exposed palm and grimly closes my hand around them.

The baby stops moving.

"But this is *God's* child!" I tell her, my palm sweating blood.

She sighs. "Just like God to send us a savior who can't be saved. He'll try again with another woman, a weaker one, not like you, one who won't stand up to him, one who'll give him what he wanted from the start—a son."

She puts her hand on my shoulder and stares out the door after her husband.

I look down at the spikes in my hand.

"He begged for mercy," I whisper. "On his knees before me, he begged *my* mercy!"

My mother's hand grows warm on my shoulder but her voice is far away.

"Yes," she says, "I'm sure he did."

THE PURE WATER GIRL

Halimat Sekula

"Pure water! Buy pure water. Cold pure water here!"

She bellows into my harassed ears. I'm torn between my attempt to find some comfort from the painfully hardened foam and tattered mock-leather seat of the aging bus, and searching for my slippery parcels. I glare at the pure water girl. Happy to be given attention, any attention, she thrusts her small package at me, accosting my nose.

"Go away girl, I am not thirsty and if I am, I would not drink typhoid infested water," I say, not too kindly of course; she adds to my discomfort in the sweltering mid-afternoon heat of Nigerian sun.

"Auntie buy? Buy pure water."

The short stocky bus conductor gives the girl's slight frame a hefty push.

"Leave! Go away. You are blocking the road. Allow my passengers to go inside the bus."

The pure water girl does not fall; she has had many such pushes in her short life. She staggers, and then steadies herself and the pail of water sachets on her head. She goes around to the other side of the bus, a package of water clutched firmly in her left hand. Come rain, come shine, or even come dust this girl must sell those sachets.

She is small—perhaps four foot eight—wiry and dark. She looks younger than her thirteen years, until you lock eyes with her. Then the brown globes grip you and hold firm, daring you to look away.

This girl's eyes tell me she is confident, daring, and unafraid to pester the most parsimonious traveler. I turn away from her formerly bright-colored skirt and blouse that hang from her small frame. Her hair, beneath the rolled bundle of rags that protects her head from the heavy pail of water, is cut to a short afro and wound into tight, unglamorous curls like so many flies on a dark fruit. She is visible proof that heavy loads constantly carried do not shorten the spine—the pure water girl's neck is a long, slender, graceful column. She evokes the beautiful woman described in the Songs of Solomon.

44

The pure water girl's left hand thrusts her pestilential goods through the bus window again. She is undaunted, even spurred on, by the competitive jostling of the forty-something year-old cake hawker and the young Hausa man tempting no one with gaudy green, orange, and turquoise trinkets.

We are in a motor park in the Yanya district of Abuja and I want to leave. Yanya is the outskirts, in fact the very hem of the skirt. Like many worn skirts, Yanya is ringed with light-brown, merciless, endemic dust—dust on my brow, dust as heavy-laden buses start reluctantly to life after sweaty pushes by drivers' boys and motor park touts. Dust wells up with the cacophonic cries of the conductors as they call out their destinations:

"Keffi! Keffi! Keffi!"

"Nasarawa! Nasarawa!"

"Jos! Jos! Jo-o-o-o-s!"

"Kwoi!"

I am jittery and annoyed by the noise. I seem to be the only person bothered. The hawkers of bread, toys, counterfeit Nike sportswear, and fake animal skin slippers are at home. The more noise, the merrier, it seems. The sweat drips from their faces onto their wares and appears to spur them into the belief that business booms. These motor park hawkers swish and glide around crazily-parked vehicles looking for the thirsty or the unwary to hoist their useless wares on.

Suddenly a motorcycle ridden by (I am sure) a lunatic, zooms into the park to add another commuter to the bedlam. Proud of the angry attention his faulty exhaust generates, the driver zooms away, a big grin under his Chicago Bulls baseball cap. The dust whirls even higher.

The pure water girl haunts this park like a persistent, restless ghost. The park is the business center for the residents of the slums of Abuja. In this slum live the thousands who subsist on the financial droppings of Abuja civil servants and contractors—cab drivers and conductors, their wives and many children, fruit sellers constantly watering fast decaying mangoes, cashew, guava and pineapples in the cruel tropical heat of the capital city of Nigeria.

These economically lower status people reside in unplanned, haphazardly assembled creations with unspeakable sewage systems. They are the men and women who would not stay in villages—their original homes—because their birthplaces had no electricity, little potable water, and little economic horizon beyond farming. So they make good their dreams of shining multi-colored lights at night and motorcars everywhere.

The city—Abuja—is the displaced villagers' dream. Their lack of formal education keeps them from getting into the many government parastatals lurking around most corners of the city center, so these people hang on to the edges. They sometimes share in the municipality quota of electricity. They buy water from vendors.

As I stare into the pure water girl's desperate eyes, a whole world appears. I shall call this girl Safana.

Safana is not from the village. Her parents are, but she was born in Abuja. Safana knows no world other than that which permeates the long trek from her family's one-room home in Mararaba through all the parks she must visit to eke out the Naira notes from thirsty passersby.

Her father is an unskilled laborer. Monday to Saturday he joins many others just like him as they line up their pans and wait for prospective builders. He earns six hundred Naira for a day's job—less than five dollars.

When the Lady of Luck smiles, father works from perhaps nine in the morning to four o' clock in the early evening. On such days of good fortune the pure water girl's father celebrates. He goes to a nearby beer parlor for a calabash or two or even five bottles of the locally brewed beer, "Burkutu." Such luck requires generosity and he does not mind buying his newly made friends a drink. To convince the rotund, dark-skinned barmaid that he will not run away after sleeping with her, he buys her drinks and some goat meat pepper soup.

Late into the night, with a crumpled one hundred Naira note still in his pocket—the lone survivor of the beer parlor experience—the pure water girl's father accosts his family with beer fumes.

"Have you people eaten?" he asks with gruff affection, as he steps over the limp, tired figure of Safana laying on the mat at the foot of the twenty year-old second-hand bed. Safana sleeps alongside four of her brother and sisters. Baby shares the bed with Mummy and Daddy.

"Yes, father." Safana and her ten-year-old brother, Ali, reply in unison. The other children are blissfully asleep.

After the silence of gathering storms, Safana's mother hisses in a long drawn-out sound and throws the proffered money back at father. "One hundred Naira! Did I not tell you baby is coughing? Foolish man, you have gone drinking and womanizing again. How can one hundred Naira feed us? Useless man, your family starves and yet every night you drink your self into a state of stupidity."

Her shrill voice rises higher with each bitter word. "Bring money for baby's cough medicine."

Baby, as if in support of her mother, starts to cough, hard. The sound touches the chords of Safana's sympathy.

Her father continues, "Woman, leave me alone! I say be quiet. Have you no pity? All day long while my peers are in air-conditioned offices, I carry pans of wet cement. Yet when I come home tired, you will not give me peace. If you do not want trouble shut your dirty mouth and allow me to sleep."

Safana hears all this and blames herself for not trekking more. Why did she stop to chat with her motor park friends? If she had tried harder, she would have made more profit for mother to buy the baby's medicine. The pain of the sorrow all around is concentrated on her slim shoulders, and seems to spare her warring parents and hungry siblings.

To Safana her mother is an angel who tries her best to manage the little resources the entire family earns. Her father's daily lamentations baffle the water girl. She wishes her father would realize his dream of a white-collar job that would enable him to wear ties. They would all be happy then.

Until her father can get a job in a ministry where no one asks about certificates, Safana will sell pure water to all the people in Abuja, in the whole world, so that her family can laugh and play like the families she sees passing in their speeding sleek cars.

Besides, she must pay her school fees. Already, her teacher, Miss Eze, singles her out on a daily basis as a perfect example of the ungrateful pupil who refuses to contribute the token amount of money necessary for her to be in primary four at the local education authority school.

Safana knows that her true saving grace, her chance at the kind of success she cannot describe in clear details, is to stay in school. She realizes that when she listens to the teacher and learns her English, arithmetic, and primary science well, she will move on to secondary school. That is her dream.

Safana attends school on Mondays through Fridays from seven in the morning to one in the afternoon. She refuses to doze for even a second in class though she woke up in the dark hours of the morning to help her mother package the pure water sachets with the small, 'Made in China' sealer. She dashes home for a quick lunch and then off she goes with her pail to sell water.

In a radio program, a spokeswoman for the Abuja Municipal Council said that in Abuja territory alone, there are over one thousand eight hundred street hawkers, many of them girls below the age of fourteen. The councilwoman mentioned the all too obvious environmental hazards of dirt and degradation caused by these hawkers and reiterated the federal authorities' insistence that these numerous hawkers be removed from the capital's territory. She spoke vehemently, 'We cannot continue to tolerate rascality."

Everyone is against Safana, even people like me. The motor park, which she has made her trading base, is littered with the ravages of her trade; polythene packs emptied of water dot the brown earth like bluish bats—ugly, unwanted, and difficult to get rid of.

Safana is unaware of the imbalance she causes with her polythene sachets; "non-biodegradable" is a term she might never hear of if her teacher insists that Safana pay all her overdue fees before she continues primary education. Her trade is the bane of environmentalists and her purpose seems subsumed in dirt.

Unlike her parents, Safana recognizes that to relent in her objective is to continue a circle that is not only strangulating in its effect on her family, but also vicious in its socio-endemic nature. Her trade keeps her parents and siblings from starving; she provides their twice-daily, mainly carbohydrate meals. Poor business for her means hunger for her everyone—an angry father, a moaning mother. Her dream of wearing a beautiful wig like Miss Eze, her schoolteacher, slips further away.

Safana's mother's roasted yam business fetches a profit of perhaps two hundred Naira daily. Any money from her mother's business is saved towards the education of Ali—Safana's younger brother.

Ali's mother, Safana's mother, hopes that Ali will grow up to one day become a medical doctor. To her mother, Safana's potential seems obvious only in her ability to feed the family. Her father does not really pay attention as long as the children are not too hungry to sleep.

Only one person truly cares for Safana—the pure water girl herself.

Against my better judgment, I purchase four sealed water packages. I buy not because I believe in the cleanliness of the water, or even that the Abuja Municipal Council's fervent wish to get rid of street hawkers is a wicked wish. I buy her water because I agree with the basics of my heroine Safana's purpose: survival and the sustenance of her dreams. She wants to be part of a happy family; she wants to be a teacher. Her father and mother have not found a way to give her a secure family life or a future to anticipate, thus she takes the future into her own hands.

Safana's fight for life, her purpose, and her paying through her packaged water trade for four years of primary education are rare. At her age, the ideal is for Safana to receive from her parents the sort of emotional and financial support she is forced by the social reality of her life in Nigeria to give to her family and to herself. She will one day, I hope, become a truly self-made woman.

Safana disturbs me as I wait impatiently for the bus to take me away from this park of madness. When I buy those sachets of probably contaminated water, Safana will not be satisfied; she will be spurred on to inflict her purpose on the next passenger, and the next, to add to her meager earnings. Most passengers do help her purpose, albeit unwittingly.

If they do not buy her water, if the federal and state governments in Nigeria do not increase their contribution to Safana's dire need of socio-economic and educational welfare, if Abuja Municipal Council succeeds in driving Safana out of the park and off the streets, if education in Nigeria still lacks books and school shoes, if Safana's father still works intermittently on a random building site, if her mother still roasts yam at Mararaba, Safana can—when she is forced to leave school before getting a certificate—take a closer interest in men, use more make-up than the little eye liner she dons now. She might become pregnant, perhaps add another girl to the turmoil of womanhood in Nigeria.

Or she might wait a few years and then find her way through myriad traffickers to Europe or America and become a prostitute and endanger the world by spreading sexually transmitted diseases. As an illegal immigrant in Europe or America, she will tax the social welfare of her host nation.

Safana does not think of these other obstacles to a good healthy future. As she eagerly lifts up that package of pure water, her ideal, her purpose, her dominating aim is to sell a little water and get a life.

TOO HARD TO TAKE

L. Howerow

Louisa Howerow

Jeannie lived in Pig Town, a hamlet whose families had small parcels of land—big yards really—where they raised chickens and if they were lucky a few pigs. The houses all seemed to be in desperate need of repair and the mothers who lived there continually pregnant.

Jeannie's mother was pregnant. Not that you could see, but I knew because Jeannie told me.

Jeannie had twelve sisters and no brothers and found herself somewhere in the middle. I was the oldest in a family of four kids and lived a mile away in Kirkland. We were both eleven, went to the same school—different classes, different friends. In the summer we drifted towards each other, maybe because we had no camps or cottages or extensive chores to keep us busy. No camps or cottages because our families didn't have the money. Few chores for Jeannie, because she managed to talk her way out of them, or so she said, and few chores for me, because my mother thought she could do things better and faster.

"Over there," yelled Jeannie. "Near the ditch."

It was August, a week before school commencement and we were foraging for smokes. I walked in the direction she pointed, and kicked at a clump of buttercups to find a squished cigarette butt. Carefully avoiding the end that had been in somebody's mouth, I plopped the prize into the used envelope I had brought along.

Jeannie didn't believe in niceties: she was stuffing her found butts into the pockets of her shirt—now she looked as if she had two small bumps growing on her chest.

"I don't think we're going to find any more." I was hot, tired, and scared somebody would catch us. Somebody meant my parents or someone who knew my parents.

"It's a lousy day for pickings." Jeannie put her hands over her pockets and cupped the contents. "Enough for half a smoke. Yours and mine together, maybe one smoke."

Smoking took place in a stretch of bush between Pig Town and the Kirkland town dump. Jeannie crashed through the trail, and I stumbled behind her, over fallen logs, past picked-over raspberry bushes, up Raven Rock. From here we could see the houses of the hamlet and the dirt road winding past them. Every yard had wash on the line, and the wash looked like the brightest, cleanest thing down there.

I passed my envelope to Jeannie and she ripped it down the sides and laid it flat in front of her. The stubs from her pockets were added to my one-stub find. We had a modest pile, better than some days, not as good as others.

Jeannie worked quickly to free the tobacco from the paper wrappers. Rip, dump, rip, dump. There wasn't much left in each stub: the people in this part of the world, including the smokers, were a frugal lot; they smoked their cigarette as close to the end as possible.

She stuck her fingers in the waistband of her shorts and pulled out a folded piece of cigarette paper, examined it in the light, and carefully smoothed it out before sprinkling the tobacco in an even line down the center.

"You want to?" she asked.

"Nah, not today."

"Suit yourself." She deftly rolled the tobacco in the paper, and sealed the long end of the paper with her tongue. Then her fingers dove once more under the waistband and fished out a box of matches.

It never occurred to me to question why I hiked the mile from home to follow Jeannie on her butt hunt. I didn't smoke. Not then. Having tried it once and succumbed to coughing and spitting, my embarrassed eleven-year-old self had decided to call it off until I was older. I know now that being with Jeannie was a safe (and for me exciting) way to fiddle with the fringes of risky behavior: I could watch, help, and still stay a good girl.

The cigarette hung thin and limp from Jeannie's mouth. She inhaled and blew the smoke out of her nose.

I tried not to wince, but the smoking trick repulsed me. It reminded me of cartoon pictures of snorting bulls. "Do rings," I said.

Jeannie smoothly changed gears, holding the smoke and blowing rings for my pleasure and astonishment. When she had smoked the cigarette as close to the end as she could, she pinched it dead and tucked the butt into her pocket.

"Thirteen. My mom s going to have thirteen. How unlucky is that?"

This had been Jeannie's line all summer. I knew about unlucky. These were all the things I learned at school: don't step on cracks or walk under ladders or forget to cross your fingers when you wished. These were all the things I learned at home: don't let a black cat or a priest cross your path. Bad luck comes in three's. Good luck can't be rushed. I wondered if Jeannie's mother was on a bad luck streak or getting ready for good luck.

Jeannie and I didn't talk much; we did things together. That summer she kept bringing up babies—wondering if my mom would have another one, whether I planned to have any.

"I don't know. Don't think so," was my standard reply, and it covered both me and my mother. It wasn't so long ago, I had learned how babies came about, and I didn't want to think about my mom doing it.

Jeannie scratched her legs and stared at her house. Her scratching was another thing that made me wince, but I kept quiet about it. Live and let live, my father would say.

According to Jeannie, her mother was sick of babies. Jeannie was sick of them, too.

"It might be a boy," I said. My mom had two more babies after my sister and I were born, both boys.

Even at eleven, I understood how things worked. If you had boys, you tried for a girl, but if that didn't work out, it was okay. If you had girls, you always tried for a boy, and if that didn't work out, people felt sorry for you. If you had neither, then everyone said your husband was a saint to stay with you. If he left, no one blamed him.

I also understood how stupid it all was, because I really wasn't planning to have babies at all. They took up too much time, could be dropped, and no one I knew was completely happy with them or what they turned out to be.

Besides, if you had too many kids, you might end up looking like Jeannie's mother. The last time I saw her, she was leaning against the gate, as if she had forgotten something—skinny, short, with a tired gray face and dark, vacant eyes. I could have been standing in front of her and she wouldn't have seen me. She reminded me of an old girl, but she wasn't any older than my mother who was thirty-four at the time.

I regretted mentioning the possibility of a boy.

Jeannie didn't say anything. She dug out a small stone with the heel of her foot and threw it towards the house.

"Your sister!" I had noticed her first or maybe I was the first to call out.

Mary, Jeannie's oldest sister, was running down the road, not it's-a-beautiful-day-for-a-run but an electrically charged there's-something-wrong kind of run. My gut told me I was right and Jeannie's gut must have said the same thing because without a word, she shot up and scrambled over the rocks. I took the path.

By the time I got down, the road was deserted; no one was in front of their house, no Jeannie, no sister. The door was closed, the curtainless windows dark, the washing bright on the line.

I had never knocked on her door and today didn't seem the best day to start. We had always met on the road to Pig Town. If she felt like seeing me, she'd go over to her neighbor's to use the phone. The calls were short: Do you want to come out? Okay. See you at two.

I waited. After a while I walked home, slowly, looking back, just in case someone would come out, or call after me, or follow me. Pink clumps of fireweed filled the ditch on both sides of the road. Usually the color alone would have made me happy—vibrant against the dark green and brown of the trees, vibrant against the dusty blank road—but not this time.

A pulsating siren sent me jumping into the side ditch. An ambulance—lights flashing—hurtled towards Pig Town. Jeannie's house. I had not shaken the feeling that something terrible had happened. Without understanding why, I stamped on the flowers, kicking and smashing them under my sneakers, and then I ran. Although I was never a runner, I ran then, feet pounding on the shoulder of the road, on the sidewalk, across streets, ran as if my life depended on getting home, being safe.

I shared nothing of what had happened. Since I wasn't a proficient liar, I had learned not to say much about my time away from home. If I started talking I'd be found out; the first question would focus on what *I* was doing. Questions were never asked before I left home, the assumption being that I was hanging around the neighborhood; the introduction of new information would start an interrogation. Cigarette smoking, merely watching someone smoke, would take precedence over the ambulance.

All through supper, I half-listened to the table conversation, took second helpings when they were offered, ate as if eating was the most important thing on my mind.

Sometime that evening, Aunt Lydia came to visit. She wasn't a relative, but according to the custom of our family and friends, the children attached Uncle or Aunt to adult visitors, thus avoiding both first-name-only familiarity and the formality of Mister or Missus. Aunt Lydia kissed my mother on the cheek, asked about the family. In turn my parents asked about hers and then waited for the litany we knew would follow. Except this time Aunt Lydia wasn't eager to talk about herself or her family. She bent towards my mother and whispered. My mother nodded and asked me to go and read in my room. I did, but I left the door ajar.

I heard about the ambulance. Aunt Lydia knew someone in Pig Town; she knew people everywhere. I heard about the blood and the white sheet covering the woman. Aunt Lydia clucked about the number of children the woman had and how the oldest daughter had run to the neighbors to phone for help. I heard about the woman's head sticking out from under the sheet, how lucky she was to be alive.

Stupid gossip, I thought, but I continued to eavesdrop.

She did it herself. (Aunt Lydia)

Do you blame her? (My mother)

Aunt Lydia was doing most of the talking, until at long last my father, who was also at the table, ushered her to the door with the excuse that I needed to be put to bed. It had been years since someone put me to bed, but I recognized the exasperation in his voice and his need to get her out of the house. Someone's misfortune had being reduced to gossip and he could not abide it.

No one had used the word abortion; but not having a word for something didn't mean it didn't happen. The stories I had picked up about sex or "doing it," were inevitably accompanied by the horror of unwanted pregnancies. If you didn't want a baby, you didn't "do it." If you were married there was no choice.

Girls or women who didn't want to go through with their pregnancies drank vile concoctions, took scalding baths, stopped eating, worked till they dropped from exhaustion, or like Jeannie's mother, dug into their insides with wires. I didn't really understand how any of those methods could work and I spent the night with my hands pressed on my belly, unable to sleep. I didn't imagine anyone at Jeannie's slept much either.

The next day Aunt Lydia brought more news: Jeannie's mother had lost the baby and maybe she wouldn't be able to have more. Aunt Lydia seemed eager to talk and to give us her opinions—the act was unforgivable, showed lack of moral fortitude.

My mother stopped her. "Maybe he should have kept his pants on." The words fell like a thud and I could see Aunt Lydia blinking rapidly, as if she couldn't quite believe what she had heard. Neither could I. Up till then, I had never known my mother to say anything even remotely vulgar.

I wasn't eavesdropping this time, but standing beside her, secretly pleased she had stood her ground. I stared quickly at my feet, afraid of looking up and smiling.

Before Aunt Lydia could start talking again, my mother grasped her visitor's hand and thanked her for coming. This was such a busy time of the year and she still had to finish sewing my first day outfit. She knew Lydia would understand. Again, she thanked her for coming by and asked if there was anything the poor woman from Pig Town needed.

We watched Aunt Lydia walk through the garden gate, probably on her way to share her story with someone else.

"Some things can be too hard to take," my mother said and turned me away from the window.

She began to wipe the counters and rearrange the cutlery drawer. I understood what her flurry of activity meant. She was telling me not to ask her about Jeannie's mother or what happened between her and Aunt Lydia.

I knew my mother was right: Jeannie's mother couldn't take any more kids. But I was also afraid. I wondered if my mother had ever found anything too hard to take. Did she ever think of doing what Jeannie's mother did? Would she have done it if there had been more of us? I couldn't imagine it, but I couldn't know either.

Would I find life too hard to take? Would Jeannie?

Jeannie and I never talked about that day. School started the next week. We kept away from each other—different classes, different friends in school. We didn't seek each other on weekends or the following summer. It was as if too much stood between us: my being with her that day, knowing how she and her mother felt about another baby.

Jeannie got her wish. No more babies. Except the wish nearly killed her mother. The wish turned into a secret—dirty, weighty, gray—and we would never be able to have our summers back, not the way we had had them before.

OCTOBER

Noah Grossman

Two kids talk.

    "The cool kids hate anyone
    who doesn't like scary movies."

One is honest.

    "I hate being scared."

The other confides.

    "I'm scared of being hated."

PROPORTIONS OF BOXES: FOUR EASY PIECES OF FICTION

Rick Castaneda

Diego

My old friend Diego used to burglarize homes, and usually I'm OK with that, but he was a thief of the worst kind. He was raised by yuppie artists. Diego broke into houses on the upper east side of a city you've probably been through on a connecting flight but have never explored outside the airport. It was one of those kinds of cities. The houses had green lawns manicured by leaf-blowing nomads, the hedges trimmed, the grass curbed, the lantern porch lights tripped by motion sensors.

Diego was a dealer in memories, stealing from the rich to sell to the poor. When Diego broke and entered, the wide-screens, the DVD Hitachi's, the crystal chandeliers remained untouched. The things Diego stole could never be bought back, never duplicated, and the family, though heavily insured, would never get one penny back. That's what made Diego so cruel.

To "move" his merchandise, Diego had a client base of about thirty to forty lonely people he'd tracked down by various ads in the personals. He searched for the ones that sounded the most desperate and least enthusiastic—the ones that smiled too emphatically in their photos or, better yet, the ones that didn't bother to smile at all. Diego tagged the loneliest and then followed them from personal ad to personal ad, cross-referencing the different dating agencies to make sure his targets were eager enough to buy his product.

Diego stole family albums, home videotapes, and diaries. He snatched love letters, bronze shoes, and mix tapes. Diego stole memories from the people who had everything, and sold to those who had none. A modern-day Robin Hood, and I loved and hated him for it. He used to show me his goods, and I'd look over them as eagerly as I would nude photos of my friend's mother, but with more guilt. I couldn't help it.

He showed me diary entries of first kisses. I thumbed through portraits of the bride and groom. Uncle Pete's forty-seventh birthday. I watched children grow up, and handled plaster casts of their handprints. I ate it all up. Here were whole lives, in the palms of my hands. He was a grave robber of personal history, and I would appraise the rings he cut off dead fingers. I couldn't help it.

I asked him, once, why his customers didn't find each other the same way he'd found them, through the personals.

"Lonely people are too picky," he said. "You'd think they'd have lower standards for personality, for beauty, than we do because they're lonely, but no. They have impossibly high standards, that's why they're lonely. And that's why they buy my stuff, because these pictures, these memories, are perfect." He tapped the paisley-covered diary I was reading. "Becky worrying about the pimple on her forehead, that's perfect," he said. "It's there, in ink, in film, on video, whatever, and it can't be changed. Therefore, perfect. These sad bastards eat it up."

He's right, too. I eat it up.

Second Guesses

My friend Jimmy had the amazing ability of conjuring up anything he wanted out of thin air, and it was always fully functional until somebody pointed out that it wasn't really there, and then it would disappear. The first time it happened I was trying to peel a banana. I'd already taken the sticker off and placed it on my forehead and everything, but I couldn't get the peel off. Jimmy reached behind his back and pulled out a banana peeler, and we were all having good times until Suzanne pointed out that there was *no such thing* as a banana peeler, and *poof* it disappeared.

The second time it happened, we were in the grocery store, buying the liquor for a wedding reception. We had loaded in about eight boxes of wine when someone asked why no one ever thought of putting wine in a keg before. Sure enough, Jimmy found one hidden behind all the bottles of wine. We were just about to pay for it, when Rich walked up from the magazine aisle. "I thought you guys were gonna buy wine?" he said. And when we explained—"They have a *wine keg?* Those don't exist!" *Poof* there it went. It had been offsetting the weight of all the other *hors 'd oeuvres* in our cart, and without it the whole thing toppled over. Baby carrots spilt everywhere. We tried to explain to management about how the nonexistent wine keg had upset the cart, but no one really understood. Jimmy hid his face for the rest of the night. It's not like we were mad at him.

The third time it happened, I was on a bus. It was only me and Jimmy this time, and we were riding the bus to my auto mechanic, to pick up my car. We were talking about sex, vulgarly and loudly so that everybody on the bus could hear that we led full sex lives, which we didn't. It was pretty late—my mechanic only works nights, which is why he's my mechanic—and I was hungry. "I wish there was a Jack in the Box on the way," I said, knowing that there wasn't. But as the bus took over two lanes to turn the corner, there it was, glimmering and shining in the moonlight. The whole bus buzzed with excitement and wonder at this newfound artifact on their regular commute.

The driver pulled over to the bus stop, which ordinarily wasn't there either, and I had one foot off the last step and falling through the air to the pavement when a middle-aged lady seated near the front wheel hub clutched her purse and called out in fright, *"There ain't no damn Jack in the Box on Third and Olympic!"* And *poof* there it wasn't.

I stepped back onto the bus, and Jimmy shrugged. "Look," he said, "There's a full moon out tonight." I looked through the fogged windows of the bus, and the moon was full and beautiful over the city. It seemed to be watching us, looking over us, guiding us. Then someone pointed out that it wasn't quite full yet, and I looked again and sure enough, it wasn't.

GR8 PL8

Carla made herself a blank license plate with magnet letters and digits she could rearrange on a daily basis. She held the tedious job of manager at a data-entry Superstore, and rearranging her personalized license plate was her *one* creative release.

Sometimes she described her mood. IMN XTC. RE5ED. 2 BLUU.

Sometimes she described her attributes. F1 LVING. BLONDI. BNG LZY.

Sometimes she described her dreams. LWYR 2B. NO1 DIVA. BRN 2 FLI.

Always misspelled, always with the creative use of digits, always the same front and back. She drove a silver Acura and lived in Southern California. She fit right in.

Everyone at the data-entry Superstore always went out to the parking lot on his or her lunch hours to see what she wrote. Carla brightened people's lives. They liked it when she put something funny, and told her so. When she put something sad, they asked if they could do anything for her. "No," she said. "It's OK."

Once she announced that she was going to write a month-long story, one word each day. All of her employees wrote her story down, word for word, one day at a time, and wondered and guessed what the next one would be. Everyone thought she was very creative, and very happy that they worked for her. The wholesale of entered data was usually quite boring, but Carla kept them all entertained with her license plate antics. "Carla," they'd say, "You should put this…" and usually, just to keep them happy, she would put it.

But then that all changed. Carla was tired of buying data-entry. She was tired of selling it wholesale. She was tired of data-entry conversations with data-entry people. She was tired of all of it. The words on her license plate began to have no connection to her life. TTH PSTE. CUSTARD. W8ING RM. Her employees rushed around her to ask what these things meant—she wouldn't tell them. They stared in consternation at her words. Why would she put "toothpaste" on her license plate? It made no sense.

With time Carla got even more upset with her job. The meaningless data that compiled in stacks on her desk began to seep into her dreams, turning them into soggy nightmares, and nonsense words began to appear on the silver Acura. Arrangements that looked like real words but weren't, not quite. Words like, "ALMRUST," "CARPERTS", and "FOGGLE." No one asked her what they meant; they knew she wouldn't tell them. They tried to guess on their own. "It's like ALMOST and the word RUST. She's saying her car is *almost rusty.*" "It's not in the dictionary." "Is it French?"

Curiosity turned to anger. They hated her for her indecipherable plates. "Who the hell does she think she is?" they asked each other over lunch. "Does she think she's smarter than us?" They kicked her tires. The quasi-words kept coming. They bent her antenna.

Carla didn't stop. She came out one day to find that somebody had keyed her car, and she was furious. In revenge she put completely random letters and digits on her car. At first her employees thought she had bought an actual license plate, and most were relieved the whole thing was finally over. But her plates kept changing, from 4YBK051 to 4PEV236 to 154HPG, and soon they all knew she was up to no good. Carla came out of the Superstore the following Friday to find her tires slashed, her windows broken, her windshield wipers snapped in half.

Carla marched back into her office and, over the loudspeaker, ordered all the Superstore employees out to the parking lot. With a ring of them around her car, she silently, slowly, cautiously, uncapped a container of gasoline and doused her Acura with it. Then she drew out a match, struck it, and lit the whole car on fire. Flames ripped across the silver exterior, from tire to hood, from brake lights to the reinforced roof. It burned, it melted, and black smoke rose from the carcass.

The crowd stood around silently and watched. Eyes shifted from the inferno, to Carla, back to the inferno again. Carla stared at the heart of the fire, and wiped some of the sweat from her brow. Somebody outside the circle coughed from the smoke.

The car burnt to cinders.

Nobody knew what to think.

Walking and Talking

We walked and talked, because they rhymed. They're grouped in countless love songs together, and that's what we were, in love. We necked by the fountain, and then went camping in the mountains, because it was the only thing that rhymed.

We did all the things our favorite songs said to do. We danced in the moonlight. We called just to say I love you. I wore blue suede shoes and she wore a raspberry beret. She took my breath away, and all I needed was the air that I breathed, and to love her.

I bought us two tickets to paradise—we vacationed in Kokomo. Whenever I was near she heard a symphony. She fell to pieces each time she saw me. And I loved her, eight days a week, and it was strawberry fields forever.

Whenever a song by one of our favorite artists appeared on a commercial, we would act it out. Bump into each other's cart at the grocery store, or simply kiss and hold each other in the middle of the street, wearing jeans. We re-enacted the Folger's Choice commercials, as well as all the other commercials where people fell in love, over coffee, over pizza, over cola, because the other had a certain car, deodorant, or clothing label.

From there it escalated. We started calling advertisement jingles "our song." Every product began to turn us on. We couldn't go shopping without getting aroused. We went on hot dates to the grocery store.

"Would you like some coffee?" she would ask.

"Desperately," I would tell her.

We started sneaking kisses in vacant aisles, then writing dirty notes to each other on the frosted glass of the frozen foods section. Everything was constant titillation, constant teasing. We spent so much time there, in such a heat, that I used to flip through coupon books at work just to get excited. I made her live recordings of Save-On Foods and put them on a CD for her, and we made love to spills in aisle seven and price checks in between the muzak.

There was no turning back. I found a gas station foreclosure in the classifieds, and we bought all the old fixtures. We paved our entire living room in white linoleum, and we had freezers, fully stocked shelves, and displays. What we couldn't buy we stole from the corner store, and after months of searching I found a scanner and cash register at a yard sale. We saved the packaging on all the food we bought and filled our store with empty containers. Then, on Friday and Saturday nights, and sometimes on Wednesday afternoons, we'd throw each other down on the linoleum floor, spilling the racks of Pringle canisters all around us. We bought bags and bags of oranges and made a pyramid display in the middle of our grocery room, only to knock it all down with our torrid, tumbling bodies.

The only trouble was the muzak, which our brains began to associate with sex. It was everywhere. In every elevator, in every department store, in every office building. It began to torment us, we were aroused so much of the time. We realized we would have to move on to survive, so we sold our grocer house, advertising it as a fully functional mini-mart, and made a substantial profit. With the money we invested in a video store a few blocks away that was going out of business. Those were very romantic days—living on mattresses in the back office, drinking wine surrounded by movie posters, and rolling around in hills of empty shrink-wrapped video boxes. It was the life.

Eventually that broke down too. We began to memorize all the dialogue from the movies we played in the store, and when we heard a line from a movie spoken elsewhere, whoosh, up went our libidos. First it was simply when our friends were quoting directly—a little "Here's looking at you, kid." or "Frankly my dear, I don't give a *damn*." But we played so many movies on the store monitors that everything anybody spoke became part of some movie. From a simple "Hello." to a "Look out!" to "I love you." Especially "I love you." Once somebody came into the store, forgot their wallet, said, "I'll be back" and we both went spastic. Every time something like that happened we would have to skip to the back room to quench our thirsts. The business started to fail, and once again we had to sell.

The market was up, our location more vital now, and we sold the rental store for even more money. And so it became a cycle; we'd buy up a business to fulfill our urges, lose all our customers, get tired of it, and move on to the next erotic thing. From video store we went to car wash, from there to an office furniture store, to a laundromat. The washing machines were great. We shied away from the food service industry, for cleanliness and safety, but everything else was open game. We turned them all into discotheques at night, and made a fortune. Our undisclosed lust for each other would make the day businesses fail, and we never paid taxes on the night businesses as we were "just having a few friends over." We'd collect back all the money we'd lost on our "legitimate" business from the government, rake up all the dough from the discotheque, and move on when we needed to.

Eventually it all led back to the music. We bought out a failing music store that was surrounded by vacant lots and even emptier office buildings, so that we could plunge it even deeper into debt and maybe build up a good bank of records for our roaming dance club. As we walked through the aisles of our newest endeavor and checked off the inventory, our eyes met as we glanced over the Frank Sinatra, the Righteous Brothers, the Supremes. We put the music on the store loudspeakers, waltzed to some of the greatest albums ever recorded, and remembered why we fell in love in the first place.

MARKED

M. Lynx Qualey

A drop of sweat bulges and tears loose from Maryam's forehead, slipping past her temple and dropping into her ear. Her eyes flicker open. She can't see the clock, but small birds are chittering, and hazy light filters through the lace curtains. Aa'med is snoring, his mouth open.

The center of her right palm throbs with prickly pain. The sheets have become tangled around her legs and she pulls at them carefully with her left hand, trying to keep her breathing slow and quiet. Once free, she elbows up on one side and uncurls her right hand against the sheet. There is a dark, liquid eye at the center of her palm. She stops breathing and tries to hold herself in, but her lips tremble and she touches her tongue to the eye. It has the bitter tang of salt. She blinks, and the eyes in her head burn with sympathy for the one in her palm. But then it's staring at her rumpled nightdress, her tangled hair, and she flushes, closing the fist.

Aa'med snores, and she climbs quietly out of bed, reaching under the bed for her slippers. She shuffles into the boys' bedroom and rustles the two of them out of bed, hushing them before they can start to whine. She strips off their pajamas one-handed, pulling shirts over their heads and yanking on clean pants. She brings them out to the reception, their hands in her fist like the strings of balloons. The TV is flipped on, and she hurries to the kitchen to make their lunches.

Ingredients come out of the fridge in silence. She makes salads and sliced vegetables and cream cheese sandwiches, even though she knows it will all come home, uneaten. Some mothers, she thinks, would just give them potato chips and chocolate bars. Or they would just let the maid feed them. But she loves her boys too much. It makes her anxious to think about the maid preparing their food, nauseous to think of them at school without her, eating food out of other children's dirty hands.

She keeps pushing the button on the water boiler, ready to prepare Aa'med's tea as soon as he stumbles out of the bedroom. She turns up her palm for a moment, the fingers half-curled, and stares into the eye. It seems to click and whir, like it's recording her movements. She buries the hand in the pocket of her nightdress, smothering it.

Aa'med makes a roaring yawn as he kicks his way out of the bedroom, into the reception. The boys jerk up in front of the television, like little rabbits. They stare at him, then at her. After a long moment, their shoulders sink and they go back to watching cartoons.

She has Aa'med's tea prepared by the time he drags forward his chair and knocks into the kitchen table with his large belly. His fingers tap the rim of the glass and he stares at her, first at her slippered feet and then working his way up. He picks up the tea and blows on it, looking at her hands, her chest, her throat. She keeps still, repeating to herself the list of items in the boys lunches, waiting for it to be over.

"What's that?" he asks, tipping his chin toward her. Her right fist squeezes shut inside her pocket.

"What?"

He nods at her, clearing his throat before he sips his tea. "Around your neck."

"Oh." A finger slips under the gold chain. It itches against her throat. "A necklace."

"I can see this. What I want to know is, how much did it cost?"

"Nothing." Her tongue is thick inside her mouth, and the word comes out slowly, slurred.

He raises his eyebrows.

"It was a gift from Auntie Yusufa."

"A gift."

The eye is throbbing inside her hand, a warning, and she keeps her mouth shut and nods.

He shrugs and looks down at the table, releasing her. He sips his tea. She hurries out to the reception, helping the boys up off the floor, kissing them, reminding them about the bus. She slips backpack straps over their thin arms and kisses the tops of their soft, beautiful heads.

A key clangs in the lock and the maid bustles in, apologizing, complaining about the crowds on the subway. She stops for a moment and stares at Maryam, her eyebrows raised. She looks down at the fist clenched inside Maryam's pocket. Then the maid bends forward, stretching out her arms. Maryam wants to yank the boys back into the bedroom, put them back in bed, the three of them safe under the covers. But the boys giggle and stumble forward and the maid takes them, one in each hand, out the door.

Sweat bubbles and itches on the back of Maryam's neck. I should bandage up the hand, she thinks. The eye buzzes in protest, pain shooting up her arm.

She slides open the glass door and pads out onto the balcony. It's cooler there, and she watches the boys appear on the street. The maid stands with them, her head down. Then the maid turns suddenly and cranes her head toward the balcony, almost catching Maryam's eye. Maryam lets go of the railing and drops to the floor. She squats and peers down through the slats, waiting until the bus comes and the maid lifts little Hani onto the stairs. Kareem climbs up after.

Maryam lingers, watching the bus drive away. She draws her fist out of her pocket and stares at it.

"Maryam," Aa'med calls.

She slides open the glass door and steps into the apartment, shutting it behind her. She hurries into the bedroom.

"My shoes." He looks at her and wrinkles his brow. He's noticed. He's noticed something is different.

Her lips tremble as she smiles and kneels down, reaching under the bed for his heavy black shoes, setting them in front of them. He stares down at her as he slips them on and knots the laces.

"Finished," he says. He bends to pick up his briefcase and then turns, going out the front door. Maryam follows him, trying to say something, goodbye, but the door closes and his heavy shoes echo on the stairs. He doesn't wait for the elevator.

The maid is in the reception, picking up the toys strewn in front of the television. The maid's eyes follow her around the room. Maryam's skin turns hot, and she slips into the bedroom, closing the door. She slowly opens her hand, and looks at the eye. It stares back at her, penetrating her deep into her blood and bones, her whole body stinging and she has to close it, hide the hand behind her back.

The maid is humming outside the door. Maryam shakes herself, unbuttoning, and pulling her nightdress over her head. Her stomach clenches and she flushes with shame, grabbing a cloth and wrapping it around the hand. Then she steps into the shower, trying to go quickly, trying not to think about being watched. She scrubs her skin roughly, using her left hand for everything.

After she is wrapped in towels, safe, she wants to looks at the eye again. She can feel it under the cloth, leering at her. Winking.

Hangers click and she pulls her ugliest blouse out of the closet and a long, lumpy skirt. This is my decision, she thinks. This means I will stay home. She pads back into the reception. The maid is scrubbing the kitchen table and she glances over, staring at Maryam's clothes, the trace of a smile on her lips. Maryam flushes.

I will supervise her work today, Maryam thinks, lifting her chin and sending her thoughts toward the maid. I will make sure everything is clean. I will organize the books for Hani and Kareem. I will make my exercises. I will polish my fingernails.

The kitchen tap shuts off and Maryam stands for a moment, exposed. She hurries back into the bedroom, pulling off the ugly blouse and the lumpy skirt, throwing them into the basket. Hangers click again, and she slides out her tight red blouse and a pair of black jeans.

She dresses quickly and hurries out into the reception, grabbing her purse and keys. The maid's eyes are on her.

Maryam's palm pulses, sending little shocks up her arm. She shuts the door behind her, closing out the maid's gaze. She can't wait for the elevator—she might be seen by one of the neighbors. She hurries down the stairs. The *bawwab* is washing down the floor. He watches as she comes out of the stairwell but she keeps her head down, walking quickly over the slick tile, not stopping until she gets to the car.

The eye is so sensitive that Maryam has to drive left-handed, keeping the right hand palm-down in her lap. She wishes she could have tinted windows. The other drivers stare into her car, honking, men winking and smiling. A bus passes and an old woman, her grandmother's age, glares into the car, shaking her old veiled head.

When she married Aa'med, she thought the people would stop staring. She thought that she'd be safe behind her husband's tall, bulky body. But from the moment she moved in with Aa'med, the neighbor women peered out of doorways, scurried up and down the stairs, telling about what they'd seen. She tried to become part of the chatter, to laugh with them, but they just smiled and nodded politely. She was always the outsider. She had complained to Aa'med, told him she wanted to move somewhere else, back to her old neighborhood in Nasr City. But he laughed and said, "This is how women are everywhere, *ya toota*. Didn't you know?"

If not for the boys, her sweet little boys, she would have gone crazy. She could disappear behind them; fade away until there was nothing left to see.

It takes almost an hour to get to Nasr City. She circles the building a few times, unsure. Then she parks on the street and keeps her eyes down as she passes the parking boy and a pair of *bawwabeen*. Her head is down, as if they might throw something at her. She can feel their stares hurling at her, sticking to her. She hurries up the greasy stairs, left palm sliding against the wall.

She knocks at the door and Yusuf is there in a moment, laughing, hands on her forearms, drawing her inside, kissing her.

"I knew it." He grins, combing his thick black hair out of his eyes with his fingers. His dark eyes shimmer with delight.

She feels engulfed in a crush of panic, like on the subway, all those people around her. She stumbles back against the door.

"What does he say?" Yusuf asks.

Her voice sticks inside her throat, then comes out in a rush, "I love you, Yusuf."

"Of course you love me, my moon. But what did Aa'med say?"

Yusuf's face is strained, his eyes popping out, and it hurts to look at him. There is a bluish stain on his floor. She touches her shoe to it. It's sticky.

"I wish you would let me clean up in here. Your maid is terrible."

"Maryam." He takes her wrists and lifts them up above her head, kissing her nose, her cheeks, resting her arms on his shoulders and wrapping himself around her. "I just want to know what Aa'med has said. Whatever it is, tell me. Did he hurt you? Did he hurt you, *habibti?*"

She nuzzles against his collarbone, burying herself. "There is nothing to tell."

"How do you mean, nothing? He can't have said nothing. He must have said something." He pulls back, gripping her upper arms, staring at her.

Her skin aches; she wants to hold something between his glare and her skin. "I can't tell him."

"You can't? You can't?" Yusuf lets go of her arms and shoves at her breastbone. He walks to the wall and slaps his forehead against it. His nose and lips are smashed into the cement. "Don't tell me this. I don't believe you."

"What about my boys?" The words are so small they almost disappear when they leave her mouth.

"Oh Maryam, my Maryam. Don't you love me?"

Her heart shrinks, tick by tick. She tries to climb back into his arms but he shoves against her chest, staring at her. His back is against the wall.

"I only want for you to be happy," she whispers.

He loosens himself from the wall and comes forward, slowly, wrapping her in his arms. She lets go, becoming soft against him. "You're weak," he whispers. "I understand this. I will tell Aa'med myself. I will just keep marking you, day by day, until he can't help but know."

Her breath comes in little pants, and she presses harder into his shoulder. "No, I—" The eye buzzes inside her fist. "I won't come back."

"What?" He laughs and pushes her body away from his. He draws his chin back, looking down at her. "What's this, my moon? You couldn't even manage such a thing, leaving me." He kisses her neck and puts his fingers against her belly, slipping down inside the waistband of her jeans.

Her skin shivers. She wants to take his hand and shove it all the way down inside her panties, to yank off his clothes, to push him to the floor and forget. "You need me," he says, quietly. "We have true love. That's why I can't bear the idea of you being with another man. Touching him. Smelling his smells."

She kisses his neck, biting, nuzzling under his ear. "But my boys."

He pulls out her blouse, unbuttoning. "We can keep your boys. We'll keep them as long as we can. And you know that Aa'med won't want them. You've said many times he never pays any attention to the poor things."

Pity washes up in her so hard that her throat aches. "I never said that. Aa'med is a good man. He tries, in his own way—"

"Stop it, Maryam. Stop," Yusuf shouts, his hands flat against his ears. "I don't want to hear this. I can't hear this."

She is quiet. Her mother-in-law is muttering in her ear, reminding her of the list of relatives to visit. Aa'med's cousin, who just had an operation on his stomach. His uncle. His Auntie Hanan.

"I love you," Yusuf murmurs. His fingertips brush against her cheek. "I am the only one who's ever loved you, and don't you say anything else right now, just don't."

She slowly opens her hand, watching him from below. Yusuf strokes her hair, her cheek. He doesn't notice the eye.

She can feel herself watching him with all three lenses, as if she had thousands of ways to see him, like a *djinn*. He had been so needy when she met him, an injured little rabbit. She had to cuddle him in her arms, kiss him to strength. She hadn't known a man could be like that, so gentle and needing. And he'd grown and grown until yesterday, when he'd kissed her hand and demanded that she leave Aa'med. He'd kissed and demanded while she giggled, kissing him back, and suddenly he'd made a strange, angry sound in this throat and yanked her arm nearly out of its socket, dragging her over to the dining room table, pressing her against the wood while she asked him, What's going on? He ignored her, pinning her against the table and reeling back, slapping her across the face. She'd run out, holding her cheek. The *bawwab* had hissed at her, and the parking boy had seen the red palm across her cheek as she fumbled with her keys. She spread makeup over her face before she went home, but her own *bawwab* had stared at her, eyes wide. What had he seen?

"I need you," Yusuf says." Aa'med doesn't need you. I need you." He kisses her neck, licks it. "Maryam, Maryam, beautiful Maryam, I need you."

"Hani and Kareem need me."

"I need you. Your boys have the maid, they have their grandparents, their aunties and uncles. I have only you."

"That's not true." She tries to pull back her right hand, her sensitive right hand.

"Who else do I have? You tell me. Give me the name."

"You can find another woman. Someone young, someone without—"

"But that's just it, *habibti*. I don't want another woman. And it's the same for you. Isn't it?"

The bare walls flicker and crowd in toward them.

"Of course."

The boys will be home from school in a few hours. The maid never fixes anything good. Maryam has to get something ready. She backs toward the door, dragging Yusuf with her.

"I'll mark your face," he says, his voice tense, strangled. "You know that, don't you? I'll give you a fourth eye. Or I'll throw acid at you if I have to. Your face will melt off and no other man will want you. You'll be a freak. Deformed. You're mine, Maryam. Don't you see that? There is no other way." She drags him backward another step, like dancing. "I love you."

He stops for a moment, shivering, burying himself into her shoulder. "Are you afraid what people will say if you leave Aa'med?" His voice is quiet, but strong. "Think what they'll say if your lover throws acid on you. You will be alone and hated for the rest of your life."

Her left hand reaches back and swipes at the doorknob, dragging herself toward the door. She yanks down on the knob and the door comes open. Yusuf springs back, smiling, combing fingers through his hair. She slips into the doorway.

He peers beyond her. "Don't just stand there, *habibti.* Your blouse is unbuttoned. Come back in."

She holds onto the door.

"I love you," he whispers. "You won't be able to live without me. It will kill you to live without me, it will be like…Close the door, *habibti.*"

She slides further into the hallway. She can feel the stares all over her exposed back, crawling angrily over her, biting off pieces of her skin, spitting them to the floor.

"Come back tomorrow," he whispers.

"I don't know," she says.

She takes another step backwards, into the hall, and closes the door. She stares at it for a moment, imagining Yusuf on the other side. She could pull it back open and fall into his arms, crying, running away with him, to Cyprus maybe. But then Hani and Kareem would wake up in the middle of the night, confused, unable to shake the nightmares loose without her. *Mama,* they call. *Mama mama mama.* She pulls herself away from the door and clicks down the greasy stairs, buttoning her blouse. She pushes through the front door, out onto the hot dusty street. Light spills over her, the sun throbbing against her eyes. The parking boy and the *bawwabs* are staring at her, whispering, hissing, clicking their tongues. They call to an old woman and a man pushing a juice cart. A crowd starts to gather.

They're watching her, clutching at each other's hands and clothes, whispering, hissing. What do they see? She raises her fist to eye-level and spreads out the fingers, staring at herself. The crowd is hissing, muttering, slithering around her. She breathes in the dusty air and pushes her arm higher into the air, turning the palm toward the crowd, staring back.

MODERN TIMES*

Daniel M. Jaffe

Daniel M. Jaffe

"Technically, Alice, according to the Torah, it's not adultery."

Alice yanks her elbow from his hand, walks down the synagogue steps, crosses the street to a park bench, sits. Bob follows, but as he sits beside her, Alice angles her body away.

"Alice," he says, touching her shoulder.

She jerks free.

"Carol's Jewish," he says, "if that helps."

"Well that makes all the difference. I'll tell you what, Bob—invite her for Shabbos dinner. She and I can take turns lighting your candles."

"I don't need crude sarcasm."

"And of course everything's about your needs."

Bob fidgets with the lapels of his medium-weight suit jacket. "It started as just a physical thing. We didn't mean for it to...evolve."

"You...you..." Alice slams a fist down onto her skirt-covered thigh. "Adulterer!"

"Not according to the Torah, Alice, not really. That's kind of why I chose today to tell you. It's not adultery according to the Torah."

She turns to face him. "What idiocy are you talking? You wear your yarmulke in bed with her? That makes it kosher? The Union of Orthodox Rabbis stamped a *hechsher* on her shapely—?"

"Alice! Stop being TV sitcom."

"It's either sitcom or murder mystery, Bob. Take your pick."

"You're in shock. I understand," he continues. "Look, we just read all about this in today's Torah portion."

She stares at him, shakes her head, squints disbelief. "You're going to quote Torah to excuse infidelity?"

"*Ki Tetze,*" he says, "prohibits a man from having relations with a woman who's married or engaged. Carol's totally single, so it's not adultery."

"But *you're* married, Bob!" Alice blurts. "For thirty years you're married!

To *me!*"

"Not a problem for *Ki Tetze*."

"Just for me."

"That's what the Torah says, Alice."

Alice thinks for a moment, then, "The Torah also says, Thou shalt not covet they neighbor's wife. Does that mean it's okay for me to covet my neighbor's husband?"

"Now that's an interesting point, Alice. I hadn't thought of that."

"For three decades I've wondered why the Almighty denied me children. Now I understand. He's kept me barren to spare our children the shame of this moment!"

"Which brings me to another point, Alice. A delicate one, I know." He shifts on the bench. "I don't mean to hurt you—"

"Of course you don't, Bob. This is all about me and my feelings."

"The Torah allows a man to divorce his wife if she's barren."

Alice stares into space, then nods her head slowly. "Of course." She continues nodding, "It's always the wife's fault when there are no children, right?"

"In our case, Alice, that happens to be true. Carol's going to have my baby."

It is this that makes Alice gasp, that triggers her tears. She wants to halt them, not to give Bob the satisfaction, but they flow nonetheless. What can she say? With which defense, with which revenge argument does the Torah arm a betrayed wife? "You know, don't you," she murmurs through salty wet lips, "that *Ki Tetze* condemns a bastard to alienation from the congregation for ten generations."

"Don't be ridiculous, that's archaic. Besides," says Bob, "my child won't be a bastard if I'm married to his mother."

Alice stops crying. Alice stops feeling. "I see," she says. "Now I truly understand." She sits quiet and still. "Divorce. I see. Of course." Then, "By all means, Bob. Anything for a child." She stands. "Well. We'll say goodbye here and now. Send the *get* Federal Express."

"Alice, I don t want to rush you, but—"

"I understand, Bob. We can't take any chances—ten generations of alienation is a long time for your offspring to be missing services. And by the way, Bob, that linen and wool blend suit you're wearing—a no-no according to *Ki Tetze*. And here's another Torah nugget I noticed today: if a bride's not a virgin on her wedding night, she's supposed to be killed. Carol needs to know that so she can pack appropriate stoning wear for the honeymoon."

"Alice, you're ridiculous."

"Actually, Bob, you're the one who's ridiculous. Although I must say I admire your comfort in picking and choosing from the Torah. I can learn from you." Alice turns away from her husband one last time, takes measured steps across the street, climbs the synagogue steps. She hesitates at the doorway, then enters the synagogue alone.

*Originally published in *The Forward*

A SLIGHT CASE OF HYPOMANIA

Anita Darcel Taylor

have a friend who insisted that she could not write without pain. I misunderstood this, thinking that she meant that pain was her subject, and indeed it often was, but that was not what she meant. She meant that when tormented, she picked up the pen and pressed its nib to the page. When she was not tortured, silence prevailed. She has since gotten treatment for her pain. She no longer writes.

It is difficult for me to conceive of the fact that I am manic-depressive. No, that is not true. I do imagine it. It is not a false reality. I am manic-depressive. When I consider all of my life, I track the illness to its budding roots, to crying jags in grade school, paranoia in junior high, peppered moments of hysteria in college. And yet, I come to the diagnosis timidly. Even nine years later—yes, it has been nine years since that diagnosing hospitalization—I shake my head vigorously as if trying to shake it away. It cannot be real. Mental illness cannot be my cross. I should be able to outsmart it.

I haven't taken medications in months. Nothing since August when I called Dr. Michaels to tell him I would return to therapy in October when I could better afford to pay. I thought that by October I could buy the medications he kept prescribing but which I kept taking on the odd days, not the even. Four hundred and forty dollars was more money than I had each month to ensure that all of my mental faculties stayed intact. If I could at least catch up on rent payments between August and October, things might change.

I got this idea of rationing from President Jimmy Carter, remembering the 1973 oil crisis. In four months during 1973, gasoline prices jumped from twenty-five cents per gallon to crest at a dollar. In order to stretch supply, Carter proposed rationing. The last digit on a car license plate would determine which day the owner could buy gas. Even number one day. Odd number the next. The nation was in crisis. That was thirty-one years ago. Today George Bush is President and, according to last night's news, in parts of the country, a gallon of gas reached three dollars. The nation is at war. I might be, too.

It is March. The clouds keep dancing in front of the sun, making my rooms go dark and then light and dark and light again as if the universe is rapid cycling. I still haven't returned to Dr. Michael s office. I won't. Too much time has passed, too little money, too. I owe him over two thousand dollars, the residuals not covered by insurance. I worry that I can't afford the cost to live. I'm fully aware that untreated, my illness gains momentum. The suicide rate is high among people diagnosed bipolar. And yet I've made a choice, an irrational one some might say, to continue buying and reading books, taking photographs, applying to university as both student and professor.

I have not returned the N75 Nikon 35 mm SLR I purchased with lens and accoutrements for four hundred dollars on a hypomanic whim, but instead have snapped four rolls of film which—for ten dollars each—I will have developed at the Ritz Camera shop on Capitol Hill, now that I enjoy a membership. Nor have I adhered to the strong recommendation of a friend and returned the lovely jacketed Modern Library edition of Proust's *In Search of Lost Time*, six volumes that I will not read until summer. I do these things rather than see Dr. Michaels monthly and buy pills. It is, I think, a choice to live despite the imminent threat that such living poses against my life.

Yesterday, I read the cover story of the *New York Magazine*. It was about the pervasiveness of bipolar III and IV diagnoses, what we used to call cyclothmia and drug-induced mania. I am either bipolar I or II; no doctor has been able to tell for sure, although the most credible among them have conceded that my lengthy history of mixed mania, rapid cycling, and hypomania coupled with at least one episode of anti-depressant induced mania and several bouts of depression and suicidal ideation probably inform a diagnosis of bipolar I.

The author of the *New York Magazine* cover story, Vanessa Grigoriadis, quoted someone—was it a psychopharmacologist or a GlaxoSmithKline representative?—proclaiming the anticonvulsive drug Lamictal to be "hot shit."

Lamictal is one of the latest mood stabilizing medications on the market. Dr. Michaels was slowly replacing my use of Depakote with it. I was pleased with his decision. Depakote hastened weight gain. I weigh two hundred and fifty pounds (give or take two), seventy of which are compliments of Depakote. Dr. Michaels said that researchers are concerned about the rise of diabetes, particularly among black patients. Lamictal's side effects do not include weight gain, a precursor to diabetes for those genetically inclined. I am so inclined. Instead there is the threat of immune-mediated illness presenting as lesions or rash, but no weight gain. I was willing to risk the rash. Being fat had brought a lifetime of shame: size B-cup by eleven years old, deemed medically obese at seventeen, manic and starving at thirty (but wearing an Ann Taylor size 10), and now, at forty-five, considering gastric bypass surgery to make my stomach the size of a pea. To do this, I would have to lie about struggles with mental health. The certified need not apply.

Seven months ago, in August, I went to the pharmacy. I had used a month of drug samples given to me by Dr. Michaels, a trial run on a new cocktail that included Lamictal, Geodon, Depakote, Wellbutrin, and Clonazepam. No problems arose. No lesions. I was stabilized. We were hopeful. Prescriptions and Optimum Choice Prescription Card in hand I went to the pharmacy window, but I couldn't afford the drugs. I couldn't afford the co-pay. I'd had it. No more buying drugs. I was fat, sometimes crazy, and perpetually poor. And I was tired. No more even-odd days. No more not buying books. No more working simply to pay the essentials. No more living impoverished and deprived. I was cashing in a life of poverty for a dance with insanity and it seemed perfectly rational to me.

The first thing to go was Dr. Michaels and his $440 associated monthly costs. With the savings, I bought a computer, a Dell 8600 wireless laptop with docking station, Axim wireless handheld, and a 15gig mp3 player— five-thousand six-hundred dollars and some change.

Next I put off the orthodontist. I spent his $450 payment on books, several of them, hard back and trade paper, classics and contemporary, fiction and nonfiction, even a spot of poetry. I read the biography of Sylvia Plath and Ted Hughes by Diane Middlebrook and bought the DVD of the film *Sylvia* starring Gwynth Paltrow. Paltrow performed all right but I found myself lusting after the actor who played Ted Hughes—the way he brushed his hand against his thick crop of brown wavy hair—which I found a delightfully ironic twist since lust evaporates as quickly as money when one is taking psychotropic. And I bought music, Irish folk and the pop of Natalie Merchant and Annie Lennox. I even caved to the hype of Norah Jones, twice.

I had my first meltdown yesterday. I stuck into my ears the mp3 ear plugs, squinting to read the tiny letters "R" and "L" that direct the user to the proper plugging into the left and right ears—I need new eyeglasses desperately—and listened repeatedly to Merchant's "Owensboro," a song about how the rich will finally, in death, be forced by God to relinquish all of their riches to the poor, also presumably dead. Martha Stewart was convicted recently, they say for lying to the Federal government but probably just as much for being a pompous ass of a wealthy woman who took advantage of what men take advantage of daily. People say she's greedy. I say she's just American. Sometimes I want to be American, too.

The meltdown was about being fat, although I'm not sure that's really what it was about. Perhaps it was about being lonely and wanting to blame that on being fat. In any case, I had a crying jag. The weepiness began as I sat cloistered in my cubicle at work. My eyes were clouded over with leakage so that the computer screen was out of focus. My fingers trembled making it hard to tap the proper keys on the keyboard I'd known by heart. It didn't matter, really. I could not concentrate, could not stop the leaking. I left work early, stopped at the Seven-Eleven Convenience Store two blocks away and bought a bean custard pie, all sugar and white navy beans. It sounds awful, I know, but is really sweet and gooey and delicious and when I got home— I hailed a cab, so much in a hurry was I to hide myself and my tears away from gawking strangers—I plunged a fork in its center, working outward until all that was left was the crust that imploded from its place on the rim of the aluminum pan. It took less than five minutes to eat. I threw the crusty part away, saving calories. I felt sick afterward, and consumed a pint of vanilla Häagen Dazs for comfort. Then I took a sedative, drank a glass of cheap wine, and went to bed. I slept well, waking at 9:30 a.m. to the rain tapping against the window.

This makes me sound like a bit of a mess. Looking at it now, perhaps I am. After all, a meltdown is never a good thing. I could blame it on the approaching full moon or my sporadic premenopausal bleeding, but I prefer to blame it on the writer, Sarai Walker.

Sarai and I are members of a small collective of Bennington writing seminar graduates who have formed a cyber writing workshop. Her manuscript is an indictment of America's obsession with surface beauty, hitting upon every nerve beneath my fat-stretched skin.

She exposes the pathological thinking that goes into penetrating and exploiting mass insecurities—we fret over our looks, compare ourselves to an image of idealized perfection, grieve our disconnect, and slave to aspire. We never reach our goal. We can't reach it, but we don't understand that we are worshipping the skeletal remains of the fashion model, and so we reach some more with Weight Watchers, Atkins, South Beach, Slim-Fast, L. A. Weight Loss as our guides. Low carbohydrates, no carbohydrates, prepackaged, and 900 calories of semi-starvation become our God of Perfection. We worship Her goodness, praying for perfect beauty the way that the poor in Owensboro pray for beautiful things. Death will be the great equalizer. At the very least, we all want to be like the character Melanie in Sarai Walker's novel, a size 2 corpse.

I put Sarai's manuscript away and picked up a drink. I touched my body, feeling the softness of my full breasts, the way they rested comfortably on the roll of fat that is my upper stomach. I felt the sweat locked inside the crease between it and the separate roll below my belly button, the roll of fat that hangs slightly, protrudes through my size 20 pants, pushing out the creases. I raised my fingers to my nose, smelled the salty sulfur smell. I never wear a belt with my pants; the leather cuts the flesh above and below, making the sweat act like an acidic coating on my skin, making me itch. Clothes are uncomfortable. I took mine off, all of them, and stared at myself in the bathroom mirror. And then I cried.

I wonder sometimes if I am an alcoholic. Once, while incarcerated at Sheppard and Enoch Pratt Mental Hospital I expressed this concern to a psychiatrist who dutifully noted it in my medical file. I was incensed. A notation of alcoholism would brand me forever. In retrospect I wondered what it was about the label "alcoholic" that I found so offensive whereas "bipolar" I sometimes wore as a badge. Alcoholism, I decided, personified weakness. Bipolar, on the other hand, is a medical condition of which I had no choice in getting but for which my choice to survive denoted strength.

My father was an alcoholic and my grandfather. The ghost of the disease is all around me, hand-in-hand with the mental illness it eases or creates, hand-in-hand from one generation to the next.

Shortly after I was diagnosed bipolar, my mother went on a research rampage scouring magazine racks and Patty Duke stories, watching news clips and exposés on the links between heredity, substance abuse, and mental illness. She knew I drank, but did I also use drugs? Was her husband's drinking somehow relevant? When did it happen, when did he turn? Was he in his mid-thirties when the erratic behavior began? Was her daughter also in hers?

She remembered a visit they made to Washington to see me. It was the summer of 1993. I was thirty-four years old. I had quit my job as an advocate for people of color living with AIDS, and I'd quit school too and was living on the first floor of a quaint little row house on Capitol Hill. They stayed with family members. I claimed my space was too small for the three of us. We visited during the day. I was distant and cruel, snapping instead of conversing, or sulking and being rude. My mother thought I hated them. She tried to stay out of my way.

A week later, when it was time to drive home, my parents stopped at my apartment to say the obligatory goodbye. They found me balled up in my futon on the bedroom floor, unable to speak, unable even to lift my head; the weight of the tears was so heavy. They begged me to allow them to take me home; they would take care of whatever it was. They would take care of me. I shook my head no, no and managed to say, "It will pass. I will be all right. It happens all the time. I promise, I will be all right." They locked the door behind them, phoned when they arrived home. They didn't speak to one another at all during the seven-hour ride. Instead, they took turns driving so one and then the other could cry.

My father is dead now, high blood pressure and strokes exacerbated by alcoholism. My grandfather is dead too. He put a shotgun bullet through his heart. Alcohol was his cheerleader. This is my maternal grandfather I should note, lest you assume that my genetic gift of mental illness was linear. What grand gestures alcohol makes to the sick among us, using its seductive powers of sweetness, fruit, and earth to strangle the mind, the body, the soul. Yet, I reach for it, for its complexity, its smooth tartness, its sweet bitter, its woody grape, the muscle and the skin.

Rarely do I get drunk anymore. I hate the loss of control, the next day's wondering about the past night's folly. But still there are times when I panic. Do I have enough money to enjoy wine with dinner? If I calculate just so, can I look forward to a nightcap with my cigarette? Why should this matter?

Why don't I quit?

Sometimes I get noble. No taste of the grape for days or weeks or months. For a time I even attended Alcoholics Anonymous meetings, but the drug addicts got on my nerves, as did the endless chatter, the dirty smells, the weak coffee. But I liked that my face was less puffy, my jeans didn't pinch. Nights were rest-filled, early mornings I scribbled in my journal. I'm healthier during those times when I don't drink; I know this and yet...

I think about Pinot Noir, Burgundy, and Bordeaux with the same caring that I think about Wellbutrin, Depakote, and Xanax. I've compared wine regions and corking years with the knowledge and sophistication that I compared SSRIs and dosages. I can afford the best of neither, the wine or the SSRI, but the cost of the SSRI far outweighs the local grocer's wine variety, so I make do.

What is this dance that occurs between medication and alcohol, between treatment and destruction, for it is true—I know it is true—that the living occurs somewhere in between. What does it look like, that living, and why doesn't it have the import, the gravitational pull to keep me centered right there in the linear gray space between the poisonous poles on each end? What prohibits me from inhabiting that space, the place where normal lives? I think about my friend, the one who gave up writing for normalcy. She mourns the loss of the writing, trying her hand at painting and film making to fill the deep gorge. It doesn't work, I think. Her painting is vibrant; no doubt her films are too. Yet still she cries for the writing, honest tears that roll onto empty pages where images can't reflect, where thoughts fail to take form. What exactly has she gained by living normally?

Sometimes I wonder if normal isn't a myth, a state of magical realism, a place of the imagination against a backdrop of lies. Is normal a thing of the middle class suburban family? Is it as chic as the gay city dweller? Is normal the adjective of the mainstream? Can I be normal with a diagnosis? Is it normal to be educationally elite yet live in poverty? Can I be normal if I'm fat?

I haven't taken medications in months. I haven't taken medications because I'm tired of thinking of myself as living with bipolar. I'm finding it's not at all hip to be a part of a mental illness trend. Bipolar is in, drugs are declared hot shit. I want out. I'm acting adolescent; I'm fully aware. I'm throwing a tantrum. I'm playing Russian roulette. I'm modeling bad behavior, behavior with severe consequences. I'm choosing to go untreated, with full knowledge that untreated, the end result is psychosis. The road to psychosis is paved with irritability, racing thoughts, inability to concentrate, diminished need for sleep, images of grandiosity, poor judgment, abuse of alcohol, denial, and, oh yes, spending sprees.

I used to get indignant with people who did such things, diabetics who shoved cake in their mouths as their toes turned black and had to be lopped off. I had no pity. Why do we smoke when we know it causes cancer and heart disease? What is it that makes exercise and healthy eating so distasteful that we'll limp with knee pain caused by eighty extra pounds of fat? Somewhere it is reported that all but 16 percent of people who lose large quantities of weight put it back on. What's so difficult about modeling healthy behaviors, popping a daily vitamin, cutting back the mountains of red meat, or using a condom when sexually active? HIV is still on the rise, even twenty years after a dead Rock Hudson forced three capitol letters out of the mouth of an American president. I spent ten of those years as an advocate, activist, educator myself. What good did it do? The last time I had sex, it was without a condom, and I haven't had an AIDS test in years.

Why would I rather have a camera than a month of stability? What is this thing called human behavior and how does it work? What is it that we really want when we dance with the devil? Is it as trite as simply being normal or is it about feeling alive?

Madeleine Albright once accused the George Bush foreign policy team of suffering from untreated bipolar disorder. Illness is often used as metaphor and although I don't appreciate my illness being likened to anything George Bush-esque, I must admit that Albright made her case that day at Tufts. Erratic behavior appears pervasive in the Bush White House. Untreated bipolar is, after all, an illness characterized by incongruity, a disorder of extremes. Elation, grandiosity, and impulse meet hopelessness, helplessness, and despair. They do a tango—the highest half of the team dependent upon and yet at war with the lowest.

The highest of extremes is a frightening place. Mania, for me, is mixed with explosive torrents of rage. Tongue lashings are reserved for those with the most demanding of expectations: that I act as a participant in the family unit, that I hold up my end of the contractual agreement among friends, or that I conduct myself in the professional manner that my employer dictates. Against them all I stomp and curse, extreme paranoia being my guide. Impulses of violence go uncontrolled; stemware flies against walls leaving glass shards on countertops, books, and chairs. Tables flip from their heels making decoratives scamper along the floor like cockroaches looking for a hiding place from the light. A physical fighting force pulsates in my chest pushing me to move, to drive if I have a car—fast and angrily, recklessly— to run, to throw things, anything with heft and weight, anything that shatters. Mixed mania breeds destruction.

And then there are the lows.

I haven't taken medications in months. I haven't taken medication since taking them did not stop me from going crazy, did not stop me from getting lost in the outside stimuli of poet Reetika Vazirani's suicide, did not ward off the pain and isolation and fear, paralyzing fear that came with news of her vicious act of madness. She murdered her son and then her self, and I stopped taking medications. I accepted that living on an even keel was elusive, that normalcy was a word that mocked me, that there was no hope, that I, too, would eventually be lost.

Pumped with chemicals that made my stomach roll twice, my thighs bruise, and my breast bubble beneath my armpits so that I could never feel alluring even if the sex drive had not also diminished, I wondered *what is this all for?* Medications taken to ward off mania and depression had gone one step too far. Medications taken to ward off mania and depression had killed any feeling at all.

I was detached, relying on memory and intellect to drive my responses to people, places and events. Empathy, compassion, joy, and sorrow were all gone. I could no more be touched, no more experience intimacy than I could fly. I could function, yes. I appeared normal enough, so that everyone around me was at ease. But I was flat, cold and void, as close to a living corpse as could be.

It is the hollowness that is suffocating. One can drown in hollowness. Medications suck the air out of life-breathing lungs just as surely as a raging river can strangle. Medications make suffocating subtle; the sufferer appears at ease. No more thrashing and flinching, she is calm, suitable for company. She can maneuver through a cocktail party or sit patiently waiting for an appointment or a bus or a movie to end. She makes no scenes. She even conjures a smile, a conversation appropriate for a dinner party. She appears normal as she moves through her mundane chores and social responsibilities. Her hollow center is invisible to everyone around her. She speaks of it sometimes, to her doctor mostly. "You need a hobby," he retorts, leaning over his notepad, scribbling new prescriptions, scribbling with the cheap pen advertising Eli Lily, glancing at the Pfizer-branded clock, and ushering her out the door. No one is concerned by her complaints of unfeeling. She is normal, they say, perhaps just a little bit bored. *Aren't we all sometimes bored?* But she is fully conscious of the unnatural nature of her muted core. And she is fully aware that it is metastasizing, gobbling up space, taking away life like too much salt water in the lungs. But the subtlety of it, the damned deceptive subtlety...*Oh she's doing just fine. All she must do is take her medicine and she will live a normal life.*

I reread this essay and attempt to conjure an acceptable middle ground to sell to the reader, to sell to myself. It must be there somewhere between the extremes of medication-induced flatness and rage or depression. How can I function well enough to work and socialize, live peaceably and happily among friends and family and write. How can I live with this disease and its cure?

Drugs kill depth. They kill intensity. The writer Phillip Lopate often talks about the thing that brings the personal essay to life, the thing he calls "thinking on the page." He relishes those twisted journeys of discovery that the essayist leads the reader on. On drugs, all of that is gone. There is no written journey; there is no thinking on the page. There is no passion, no thinking at all. Is that what happened to my friend? Perhaps it wasn't that she required pain in order to write but that she required feeling. Sometimes any feeling is better than none. At least then you know you are alive.

I used to wish that I was more like so many people around me, people that live on the surface, consumed by a simple daily life of sitcoms and the oxymoronic reality television program. But I am not. While not an intellectual of the coveted New York variety, I can't seem, even when drugged, to find myself in *Seinfeld.* Instead I start to itch that I can't think, can't focus, can't concentrate to read or watch a movie or care about what the Bush administration is inflicting on me. I cease feeling music, hearing poetry, or seeing the seasons, and it bothers me. I stop being moved; my eyes are deadened dry.

There is relief in this sometimes, of course, especially after a bitter cycle of depression when the only thing felt is excruciating pain, when my stomach sickens at having to wake each morning, at having to bathe or brush my teeth. Then desperately I want the drugs, all of them, the whole cocktail by the fistful. I don't want to die. Even when suicidal, I don't want to die. I want, instead, for the pain to stop. And so I take the pills and I level out: the kitchen is clean, my sheets are fresh, the air is sterile and for a time, sometimes for years, I am satisfied. This is better. I tell myself I can exist this way. Book spines stare at me from their shelves, and I tell myself that I don't have to pick them up. It's enough that I used to be able to read them, that I still know what's inside their jackets. That knowledge does not leave. I have my memory, after all. I remember when I had a life, had a self, and I make myself content with that. But then, something will happen to jar me, to shake me loose from this complacent and drugged state and I'll need so much more.

When Reetika killed herself and her son, I was awash with anguish and fear. It had only been a month before when I met them. Then I was frantic and paranoid and quickly breaking down. But I was feeling. I was human. The shock of Reetika broke through my medicinal barriers, and, as a result, I was alive. Much as she was dead, I was dangerously alive. I could mourn and grieve. And I could write. Writing, thinking on the page, was electrifying. I was flooded with emotion and it poured through my fingers to the keyboard, to the computer screen, where I could see what I thought, witness feelings, my feelings. It was painful and ugly, frightening and morose, and I was swallowed with such force that clawing at the surface did nothing to pull me out. Still, better to feel pain than feel nothing. Better to be able to communicate that pain than communicate nothing authentic at all. I thought about my friend. It was torturous pain that brought her pen to the page. Without it, she was silenced. I was beginning to understand.

As a little girl, I worried about all the things prohibited me by my religion. I ruminated on the limitations wrought by a good Christian life. Excess and worldliness were so much more appealing than the Godly life. I reasoned that if He were a forgiving Lord, he'd forgive me even at the last, at that point before dying, those seconds between when the bullet hits and the last breath is taken. The point of repentance was just before dying, and God, the forgiving God, would certainly forgive me.

My gambling strategy has not matured. I will go without medical treatment until threatened. Taking my own mental health pulse, I will avoid Reetika's fate by tuning into the hypomanic warning signs of lack of sleep, irritability, alcohol abuse, and excess spending. In the meantime, I will enjoy what other people enjoy, unmedicated normal people enjoy: laughs that come from somewhere deep beneath the belly, vivid dreams and the occasional nightmares, energy, an attention span long enough to enjoy a movie or read a delicious novel from cover to cover, preparing a meal, savoring a perfect pot of tea, or all the other everyday human ordinariness. I am smart. When it all turns sour, when the ugliness peeks its head, I will know.

My dreams have been lovely. I had forgotten what it was like to wake from a sleep-filled dream, to be in that half-place where you're not sure if it was real—the flying you did that night, or the lovely visit from your dead father, or that nap you took with your first boyfriend, or the orgasm. Oh, the orgasm. How long had it been since my body convulsed in that perfectly pitched musical way to its own rhythms, its own dance? How long had it been since I'd loved my own body?

Manic depression is more than a small inconvenience. Ragingly manic or suicidal depressive: at its extremes the disease is like the Mississippi rising after days of heavy rains. The rains fall, the river rises and waters run, breaking dams and levees until valleys turn to seas crushing homes, crushing worlds, crushing people. There is no stopping a swollen river. It works methodically day after day of continuous feeding until finally it is stuffed and bursts to exert itself, forcing itself violently through the barriers erected weeks and months and years before. Manic depression doesn't like being contained. It gets angry when we try to shush it, to cage it, trap and transform it into something innocuous and bland. We are trying with our drugs and therapy to transform it into something else, something it cannot be, and it resents us for it. It is wily and smart, knowing it can never be eradicated but resenting our trying. It nibbles on the tiny kernels we drop—money worries, lonely moments, rejection slips, failed diets, missed pills—until a feast presents itself, a feast like news of Reetika's murder/suicide. Then it has all that it needs; it has the energy of the Mississippi, the energy to break through.

Knowing all of this, why am I offering myself up to this disease? I stopped taking medications because…because what? I stopped taking medications for no noble reason at all. I stopped taking medications because I could, because no one was watching me, because on the first day of skipping them, I felt fine; and on the second day, I felt fine; and on the third and the fourth and the fifth days, I felt fine. And then I began to feel better than fine. I began to dream at night, nice dreams of being touched by someone, a man. And I remembered that touch from before I was sick, and it felt good to be held in his arms, lay my head on his shoulders, smell the brown of his skin, feel the tips of his fingers move slowly, freely, lightly against the nape of my neck, the back of my head and I wanted that dream again, to feel what waking hours did not bring, to feel the sensuality that drugs erase.

I shed lethargy when I went drug-free. I didn't need to sleep eight or nine or ten hours each night. I could participate in evening activities and actually be engaged, could sit through a reading without glancing at my watch, without yawning, without being cranky the next day for lack of rest. And what's more, I could get excited; look forward to an hour of Doris Lessing or Grace Paley; turn an hour with Lynn Sharon Schwartz into an evening of book shopping, dinner, and a nightcap with a friend. I could do what normal people did on Thursday nights, Friday nights, Saturday, and Sunday. I could live.

My writing was stronger without the medications. It had more depth, more passion and impulse. My writing had a rhythm. It was like me. When I didn't take drugs, I turned on the music and danced; I danced in the mirror, I danced on the page.

The medications betrayed me. We had an agreement. I would be compliant, and they would make me normal. We altered our agreement. I would be compliant, and they would keep me from getting sick. But then…I was compliant. They allowed depression to break through. I saw my doctor. We changed my drugs. I took them for two months. I stabilized. Then I abandoned our agreement. I had gotten the refreshing taste of feeling and was happy, sad, angry, confused, bitter, outraged, lonely, and I was dreaming.

But now the sourness is coming. It is time, I think. I must return to the damned devilish contract. I must begin again to swallow the mood stabilizers, anti-depressants, and anti-psychotic medications that dull me. This time I will buy them from Mexico for a fraction of the price. The dancing will stop and the dreams, like the men, will go away; the energy will wane, and I'll have no desire to walk to the park or the metro or the corner store. I won't have the impulse to clean. Writing will become difficult, reading a chore. But I must sign the contract in spite of it because following the lost touches, the spring walks, the silly purchases—cameras and books—comes something ugly, something urgent, something like the rains, like the river, something like destruction. Vacation is over.

"TOO MANY SALTINE CRACKERS WILL DRY OUT YOUR MOUTH"

KRISTI SWADLEY

Kristi Swadley

he tried the. old trick imagining.
his audience. naked. it backfired.
horribly. he tried going to his happy
place. remembered with a. frown.
he didn't have one.

his father used to tell him. son. if you
want. to be heard. you have to speak up.
he left when he. was eight. he was
a. bastard. his advice went ignored. good
or not.

his aunt was an. abusive drunk. his uncle
a. small beaten man. literally. she domineered.
every holiday dinner. he's pretty sure she.
hated him. because he was a. boy. he was
afraid of her.

his first girlfriend finished his. sentences
for him. even if she went off course. they
became hers. she convinced him he was.
in love. with her a. one night stand. proved
to him. otherwise.

his best friend. came round when he
needed something. he once wrecked his
car. promised to pay. for the damage.
when he got a. job. he never did. either. he
died in '86.

his first marriage was a. new generation of.
his aunt & uncle. the union bore a. child.
he wanted different. for the baby. the divorce
was when he first. realized. there was a.
pattern to his life.

she got the girl. he visited her. on occasion.
his daughter became a. dollar amount.
her mother's insistence. of course. his
only love got a. new daddy. mommy's
new lapdog.

his second marriage was. better in a. sense.
she quietly. manipulated him. slyly controlled
him. never raised her voice. her fist.
she casually drained. his accounts. his life.
his manhood shriveled.

he filed chapter 11. lost all visitation.
rights. watched his baby grow. on the
glossy. fronts. of. christmas. cards. he detached.
deteriorated. drew a. cocoon around himself.
a lowly caterpillar.

he contemplated. suicide. life as a. drunk. beach
bum. hermit. he thought he might seek. revenge.
didn't know. how to do. it. who to ask. for help.
his mother.died the day. he resolved to see her. for
the first time. in 12 years.

his uncle died next. somehow managed. to
save money. behind his wife's back. had taken
pity on. his nephew. left it all to him. his aunt
failed to. contest it in court. he marveled. the
old man had. deceived.

he couldn't. figure out what. to do with.
his newfound small. fortune. didn't spend
a. dime first. 3 months. didn't even cash.
the check. just stared at. the zeros.
mused to himself.

he took a job as a. librarian. his mom had. paid
for a. degree. in english. he thought it a. small tribute.
dreamt of one. day erecting a. library in her name.
maybe he would do that. had the money.
yes. maybe.

he paid his bills. ate when he remembered.
rode a. bike. never bought a. car. frequented
dollar stores. avoided luxuries. saved every other.
penny. his inheritance was. supplemented. nicely.
he smiled.

he often walked home. when it was warm. he walked
into his first. ex's husband who. was now her. ex.
she had developed a. drug habit. daddy 2 was worried.
about his. step. daughter. hoped daddy 1. could do.
something. about. it.

he could. he did. she put up a. fight. too
strung out. no one gave a. shit. his child was
his. again. he brought her into his. new apartment.
she refused to speak. ate little. one day she said.
daddy.

his daughter grew. happily. learned to like his. third
wife. they gave her a. baby brother. he realized. he
was happy. knew he had worth a. voice. became
a. teacher. he was fond of. poetry. today is his.
first day.

he looks out over. expectant faces. his students.
naked trick. long. forgotten. lost his voice.
found it. again. said. hello. they responded in. kind.
ghosts died. that day. so did a. small. beaten. man.
he smiled again.

SCULPTING

Debbie Ann Ice

remember the exact moment my future left me. I can still see the claustrophobic, antiseptic office, mere yards from rooms filled with listless bodies, hopeless cases. Dr. Dresner was at the hospital making his rounds and asked me to meet him after my blood tests came in. He said my results couldn't wait for an appointment in his off-site suburban office.

I had told my husband I simply had a small cyst removed from my arm. "You never said anything about cysts. What cysts?" He put down the paper, something he rarely did when he made it to the sports pages. I said, a bit too flippant, "I've had it all my life. No big deal. It's getting in the way of my tennis serve." I giggled and refilled my cup with coffee. My lying was instinctive, like grabbing your child's hand at a street corner when a car speeds by. I couldn't do it to him, couldn't make him go through all the trauma—clinging to hope that's more like fantasy, praying to a god he felt like hating; lying to children who still believed in Santa Claus.

Dr. Dresner's voice was sympathetic but clinical, which soothed and annoyed me at the same time. "The cancer may have metastasized. Your LDH is quite high and the blood tests indicate potential involvement of the liver. This is the problem with non-Hotchkins lymphoma, as I discussed with you. It can be aggressive."

I insisted he give me the dreary statistics. I had a 70 percent chance of being around next autumn. I tried to picture myself under my Japanese maple as burgundy leaves fell about me and collected at its gnarled roots. There was a 50 percent chance I would make it to winter. I now saw my frail body, wasted inside oversized wool, standing at my steam radiator, sipping coffee, as I watched bits of ice swirl in the wind. There was a mere 30 percent chance I would make it till spring. I saw my children grabbing eggs under my azaleas, their buds tight ready to explode into color, as I watched from the hammock. Those numbers leapt to 100 percent, 80 percent, and 60 percent, respectively, if I pumped medicine into my arm that would make me vomit, lose my hair, and lie in bed frail and listless. I liked baseball hats, but the thought of wearing one eternally while my body shrank into a shadow was not appealing.

"Susan, we're going to have to begin chemotherapy right away." Dr. Dresner walked over to the file cabinet and started pulling out information on drugs, all in glossy pamphlets with quick summaries written in that medical coldness, edited by lawyers who made sure every possible horrendous side effect was mentioned so as to keep insurance premiums down. "And I think you and your husband should talk about this together. He needs to be in on your decisions." I said nothing.

Dr. Dresner continued, sounding like a motor in neutral, puttering out hope here and there between information necessary to lengthen my time in his care. Oncologists immediately take you over as if cancer has passed your life title certificate to them. They talk about all the things they're now going to do, all the people you're now going to see, all the options you're of course going to explore. Live. They all want you to live. Swallow pills, insert needles, lie under blasts of radiation, so you can breathe a few more breaths while your family became filled with false hope and huge bills. I heard him the way one hears a radio turned on in an apartment across the street.

I stood up and walked towards the door. He kept talking. "Susan, this is a shock, I know." When I opened the door and left, he finally shut up; I only heard the phone ring at the reception's desk and my leather soles slapping the yellowing floor beneath me. I wanted out; I wanted air; I wanted to see a world that was fading.

After a week of reflection, I called Dr. Dresner from my cell phone. I was in my SUV flying down I-95, heading somewhere. I told him to forget chemotherapy, and after interrupting him several times, demanded he not breathe a word of my condition to a soul. He insisted my family know, so I reminded him that if they found out I would sue him all the way to a trial with jurors picked from a community fed up with watching his Mercedes poke around town.

I don't think scared accurately describes my emotions. Terrified isn't quite strong enough either. I never had the false sense of comfort associated with the belief in fantasy. I was quite sure there was no white tunnel filled with angels waiting for me. No, if there was a tunnel, it was dark and lonely. But my greatest fear had to do with what my death meant. Once the lights went out, my life would finally be defined. And what had my life been but a series of obsessions and mistakes?

For three years I had studied pottery. Pottery! I had taken classes at the town art council. You'd think a class per week would be enough, maybe culminating in a few planter pots for my living room. But no, I went on. I made my own clay: English clay, domestic china clay. I even moved on to more specialized clay: bentonites, carbonates, and phosphate-based clays. I glazed my own pottery and used a kiln at a nearby college. I even organized a pottery chat room on the Internet. My art filled the garage, rising up and around the perimeter like The Great Wall of China.

"What the hell are you going to do with this? Can you sell this shit?" Dan asked as he helped me stack my pieces. He was forced to move his gardening tools outside in a wooden box covered in plastic. We hung my boys' bicycles from the garage ceiling and stuffed all outdoor toys in the attic. Half the playroom had been converted into my sculpturing room. I smiled and told Dan that it was very hard to get to that gallery level of art. I was almost there, and my teacher thought I was one of the most talented pottery makers in the class. I was also by far the youngest. One classmate was over ninety. I was always worried when she missed a class.

Art takes concentration, so managing the children had interfered with it on occasion. Guilt also got in the way. Once, while I was molding yet another cylindrical masterpiece to add to the garage gallery, I forgot about David, who was three at the time. He was in the preschool director's office when I finally arrived to pick him up. I was over an hour late. "We tried to call, Mrs. Riley, but we just got the answering machine." I turned the answering machine on when I worked on my art. "And you never filled out the emergency form, so we didn't know who else to call," the pudgy, self-satisfied director said in that tone that screamed "bad mother." I took David to the park to calm him down. After we came home, and David got comfortable in front of "Barney," I finished my pot.

Somehow, with my future gone, my pottery looked silly. A week after my death sentence, I stood in my garage for almost an hour, staring at my definition, my entire essence—pots. Cracked, crooked, empty pots.

While I lost my future, my family still had one, so I turned my attention towards rearranging it. It took two weeks to remove the bowls from the garage. I placed them in storage. I figured the children may want them some day as memorabilia of their strange mom. I put my boys' outdoor toys back in the garage along with Dan's garden tools. I stacked Dan's fertilizer, small shovels, and hoes neatly on shelves I had installed for him.

"So, you finally sold the pots?" Dan had come home early and stood in the garage a good fifteen minutes, staring at the boys and me as we organized the gardening tools. He had finally realized something was different about the place.

"Well, pots take time to sell. I put them in storage until I get my marketing plan underway." I smiled, put a shovel down and stood back, raising my hands at my creation.

"Yeah. Are you going to research marketing chat rooms now?"

I poked him in his side and slid both arms around his belly, fastening them with interlocked fingers. I loved the soft swell of his torso that breathed under the weight of my arms. I squeezed hard. "I may have to move on to advanced classes first. Those classes have really old people. I mean sometimes they hold it at the funeral home."

"That's sick." Dan chuckled and looked down at me, trying to catch my eye, but I didn't look back. I could never let our eyes linger, not even at night when I sat on top of him in what sometimes felt like furious sex. I made love with my anger and hunger for life, keeping my eyes closed. I could only die with my plug in place. His eyes unplugged me.

Once the pots were removed, I concentrated on the children. Every time I contemplated their motherless existence, I dissolved into tears, and decided I had to fight this disease and win. But when I considered challenging my monster, I realized how slim my chances for survival were. My children would end up filled with memories of me wasted away in bed. No, it would be better to set up their future as quickly as I could, then figure out how to do away with myself. In the mean time, I would educate them so they would remember me as an alive, wise woman, not a dying, pitiful lump in a musty smelling bed.

I was so anxious to leave my last marks with Charlie and David that I annoyed them. "Why can't I go to Luke's house? I want to play basketball at Luke's," Charlie whined as I led him and David out on a nature walk down a path around the pond in our back yard. I don't know why I dragged my children into the woods, risking deer ticks, Lyme disease, poison ivy. I wanted to teach them thoughts they could tell their children some day when asked about their grandmother. I said, "All these things connect, you see. The oak needs the squirrel to distribute acorns. The flowers need the bees to take the nectar." David, the four-year-old said, "Don't squirrels eat acorns?" I said, well, of course they did and tried to think of why that was good for everything else. Charlie, my eight year old, said, "Mom, bees use nectar for honey? So how is that good for the flower?" I couldn't quite remember what was good for the flower, so I moved on to something else.

The children did more than listen to my thoughts everyday; I still had play dates for them. I'm not sure the other children appreciated my interference. I always made David and his friends play games that required cooperation. I had picked out several things that were important for their survival, and cooperation was high on the list. "David, this is how the world works—cooperation," I said, shifting my eyes to Henry, his frail friend from down the street. I opened the carton of eggs and placed it by his feet. Egg tosses were a noncompetitive way to show children this theme—that life isn't doing things better, it's finding ways each person can do their best so that the game can continue. David and his friend giggled, which interfered a bit with the accuracy of their throws. I stood by David. "See, how you have to throw it softly and you, Henry, have to catch it just so. Each has to do his job." I felt so wise, so important. When the egg fell on Henry's shoe and oozed around the shoelaces and onto his socks, David cooperated by picking a few eggs out of the carton and throwing them on his shoe. This led to several other cooperative gestures: squashing eggs on shirts, pants, and finally Mommy. But I think they got the point.

While I worked on planting maxims in the boys' heads so their mommy would exist forever in small sections of their cerebral cortex, I also spent time looking for the perfect *au pair*. My children simply had to have a mother. I told Dan I needed help so I could take some extra art classes, maybe volunteer more in the community. He agreed. "You've looked a bit frazzled and tired lately. Take a break. Do some stuff out of the house."

Actually, I admit I had always wondered if the children would be better off with a replacement. If there were such a thing as a Mommy boss, I would have been fired long ago. I just couldn't go with that child-rearing flow. I always became quickly flustered. I was unorganized, messy and a slow thinker. I sat and thought so long about what my kids did, they were completely out of control by the time I figured out what to do to calm them down. Good mothers think fast. I never should have gotten the job. This, of course, was why I had given up and found other things I could do—like make clay bowls.

Silgrid entered my kitchen as if she had been in it all her life, as if every sticky fingerprint was already known and accepted. She was a twenty-two year old Swede, just out of school, eager to see our country. She had a green card and planned to stay in the States for at least three years. She was intriguing looking—blue eyes, Greta Garbo cheekbones, auburn hair, a body that was solid, well-fed with good food that makes cheeks ruddy. And she laughed— not a soft giggle but a hearty, genuine explosion of enjoyment. I loved her.

"Charlie is a funny boy," she said as we sat on the patio that overlooked our pond. I chatted with her the first day, trying to get to know her more intimately before she took over my children. Charlie stood by us while we talked, interrupting with his own set of questions. "Is Sweden on the other side of the earth? Is it cold? Are there bass in Sweden? Do you fish?" He couldn't ask her enough questions. He finally walked off with David to toss stones into the murky water. She looked out at the boys, both balancing on the edge of a large rock by the pond's edge. "Charlie always starts questions by raising his hand. So polite." She looked at me for acknowledgement. Maybe she wanted a funny story about other times he had raised his hand inappropriately to question something, or maybe she waited for me to sim- ply say, "Oh, I know." But I said nothing, just smiled. I hadn't really noticed this trait before. She continued. "And he knows so much about your pond, all the different fish. He reads about fish, no?"

"We fish a bunch," I said. I had only fished with them once, and that was over a year ago. I hated the worms and the hooks that got caught in the fish's eyes. It was all so awful. Charlie learned to fish from his Dad and practiced a few times a week with friends. I worked on my pottery and observed them from the window.

"Charlie said that bass are hard to catch. Bass are a very unusual fish to have here, no?" I nodded, not really knowing, just wanting to go with the flow. Silgrid smiled. "This is all so beautiful. You're lucky to have all this—the pond and fish. You must be a rugged outdoor woman, yes?"

"I'm a ragged woman who likes the sun. Is that the same thing?" Her laughter put me in such a good mood. I had been weak all morning and could hardly leave my bed.

As my monster took hold of me, creeping around my insides, reminding me of its presence with fevers, diarrhea, and lethargy, I slipped into a state of repine. I would lock my bedroom door, sit in front of my mirror and stare at my sallow face. I was shedding, like my deciduous trees, but what fell to my feet was still alive and green. The loss of the world around me was worse than the loss of myself.

I withdrew from the children, allowing more space for Silgrid to bond. Sometimes I followed her around the house, listening and observing as she cleaned up and chatted about the children and their days. She was like an antenna, picking up obscure noises hidden in clues that lay in unlikely places. She transformed my children into something my scrapbooks never quite captured.

David had always been a boy swallowed by the earth and its squiggling creatures, filled with questions that reflected a rather annoying curiosity. He used to ramble on behind me as I fumbled through household chores. "David has a different language," explained Silgrid. "He is eccentric and wise, you see. He use insects to find out about life." We were having tea in the kitchen, watching David through the bay window. He was digging in his dirt hole, lightly brushing back the yellow, orange and red leaves to complete his work. Silgrid said, "When he asks 'are bees happy?' he is curious to understand if things that sting can be happy, you see. He is interpreting the world." She sipped her tea and paused a moment to take in David, soiled from chin to knee, digging furiously in his dirt pile. "He is like you, yes? An artist. Gathering the world and putting it all together. Very wise boy." David pulled out a long earthworm and rolled it between his thumb and forefinger.

Charlie, my eight year old, was a closed box, lost in his own world, obsessed with things. I had pottery; Charlie had a coin collection. Silgrid said, "I ask him about his pennies. That is how you tell what happens to him at school." We were sitting on Charlie's bed, which was covered in a new brown and white striped blanket. He had told Silgrid the colorful airplane comforter that I purchased (it went with the wall paper) was a "baby blanket." I gave her permission to take him to the linen store the next week. The brown blanket didn't quite go with the blue and white walls, but who has cocktail parties in the children's room? What had I been thinking?

Silgrid opened up his coin book and talked as she looked at the pages, "He talks a lot about these small pennies. See these on top of the quarters? All the small ones lined up at top, the large ones at bottom. See here?" She pointed to one page with old brown coins framing the top. She closed the book. "He tells me about school after we discuss these. He's so small, but he's a very brave boy. He defends himself on playground. He raises himself above those big quarters." She pulled her chin in and chuckled. I never knew Charlie was being teased about his size or that he was brave. He just said "nothing" when I asked what happened at school each day.

When Silgrid left the room, I stayed on the bed, holding his book close to my chest like a newborn baby.

I was fairly confident my children would be fine, actually more than fine as long as Silgrid stayed a while. But dealing with Dan became increasingly complex. I couldn't stop thinking about my barrel-chested, hairy, quiet man with another woman. I had never wondered about what other women thought about him; we had merged so tightly into one. Where would he end up when I was gone? Who would he find, and what would she be like with my children? I cringed at the thought of her touching him, driving my kids to school, hugging them goodbye. But the image of my family alone was worse. Silgrid may stay on for two years, but eventually my children needed someone else.

I split in two, one side pulling Dan in, wanting him to hold and comfort me, the other half pushing him away from any view of my pain. While I had no intense physical pain, my malaise interfered with our life. Needless to say, my appetite for sex waned. I was no longer ravenous for him, but tired, listless.

"Susan, you're losing too much weight. Why aren't you eating?" He finally said one night. The kids were down for the night and we were having a late dinner. He picked at his food, drank water instead of Merlot, and leaned into me when he spoke, as if I had a hearing problem.

I smiled and struggled with the cheesecake that had no smell and tasted like sweet cottage cheese. "I'm just trying to look like an upper middle class woman."

He didn't laugh. Gone were our quips, pinches, self-deprecating asides. He became careful, paternally affectionate, sometimes holding my hand as if I were a toddler.

His attention didn't sit right, and I didn't want to accept it. This kind of affection felt painful, embracing it, selfish. I wanted him away, removed, before I broke down and confessed. So I became a bitch. I always had bitchy thoughts, particularly since I had discovered I was fading away, so the behavior came naturally. I yelled over nothing, things I used to laugh about—kids accidentally dropping eggs as they baked with Silgrid, Dan tracking mud on our already soiled carpet, underwear on the floor. "Why don't you ask about my day?" I said when he started an office anecdote. "Your day actually bores me." Dan slammed the den door so hard it cracked.

I thought all of this would work; I would fade into the walls, push my kids into the nurturing arms of an attentive Swede, nag my husband away from me. My death would be this wonderful thing after the shock wore off. They would cry, of course, but then, eventually, everyone would realize the world was a happier place. But no, after the screams and slammed doors, Dan would stare at me again, sometimes for days, then arrive home from work with flowers and a smile. The thinner I looked the more attention he gave me. I started drinking soy protein shakes to put on weight. I gained maybe two pounds. Dan followed me around, helped out with the cleaning, cooked meals when I looked particularly run down. My push away plan didn't work; nagging didn't send him away into another's arms, but instead made him someone who touched, cooked, and helped with the laundry. I needed to write a marriage book. "Bitch Your Husband Back into the Household."

Then, just when I thought my children had bonded with another, they, too, became constant companions, sounding off at my closed bedroom door, wanting a band aid, a hug, a question answered. Charlie, the mumbler, metamorphosed into this chattering Momma's boy. David brought worms to me, telling me they were sad, but still happy. I didn't know what to do, how to leave the world. I couldn't push them away; I didn't want to do anything but hold them so tight they would curl back into me.

And the pottery questions never ceased.

"I thought you stored your pottery to free up room. You needed all this help to study more? So, what's with your art? Where's your clay?" Dan pushed his eggs around his plate, his eyes on my hands that now shook as I lifted the fork to my mouth.

I forced my jaws to chew my food, then sipped my protein shake. "I do my pottery at school." I grabbed the paper as if an article was reaching out from the page pulling at my hand.

Dan poked an egg like it was an insect he was killing.

For three years Dan had whined about the unorganized house, my wasted time, pots pushing everyone else's life into a corner. Now that the house was in order so I could wither away guiltlessly, everyone clung to me and wanted me to mold pots. Even David became obsessed with my clay. He started playing with Play-Do. "Mom, did you lose your clay? You can share my Play-Do, and we can make something." He chattered daily about his Play-Do creations, all worms of various sizes with frowns scratched on their faces. Sad worms.

What the hell. Over the next month I got out my clay and worked, molding faces of my children into elaborate busts. I didn't realize how much I missed the clay, how hungry I was for it. I sculpted Dan's head too. My children were thrilled and helped me every afternoon. I even gave David some clay and he molded a few worms. Charlie helped with Dan's head and eventually made a few pots himself. For some reason, his pots never cracked. Silgrid stood by as we worked, occasionally chipping in, cleaning up, but mostly staring at me.

I was peeking out my bay window as my family built a snowman when Dr. Dresner called with the monthly test results. I had promised him I would undergo tests at least once every two to three months. It was the only way to shut him up. "I couldn't wait till Monday," Dr. Dresner said.

I had been thinking about packing up and taking off so I could die somewhere away from this precious world now clinging to me. I just needed to take everyone in one last time.

"This is unusual, Susan. Only seen this happen once before. Please reconsider chemo. The cancer has stabilized."

Dan threw a snowball high up high in the trees. Both boys screamed. David ran after Dan. I studied David, how his hair flopped upon his brow lightly, unnoticed by him.

Dr. Dresner continued, fast and excited. "This is quite encouraging. You're a great candidate for chemo. Please, Susan, reconsider."

I leaned against the doorway and sipped my Chandan tea, something I found at a health food store.

"Susan?"

Dan turned toward my giggling boy, arms up, hands bent into bear claws, roaring, being silly, as usual. Silgrid sauntered away to pick up some more snow. When David jumped on his back, Dan turned towards the window and looked at me.

I heard Dr. Dresner breathing, waiting for me to tell him I would fight for my life, even if that meant only a few more years, a few more clay busts, a few more Play-Do worms. I continued to stare at a family that seemed to be in perfect sync, one that would survive just fine.

Charlie let a snowball fly, and it hit Dan right in the middle of his face. Dan stared at me, then raised his shoulders into a parent shrug and smiled, his lips turning up into the usual crooked curve. Dr. Dresner said my name again, but I said nothing, just lowered the phone and took in the view: my children, out of control, delightfully in their element; the pond, covered with freshly fallen snow; Dan's eyes communicating to me in the familiar way that said, "Look what we've done, Susan. Look what we've done."

A GIFT FOR EFFECTIVE LANGUAGE

Max Sparber

My desk is cluttered with panicked memos about the television show. There is a problem with the talent. In particular, the actor playing the main character, a golem, insists on whining and stuttering his lines as though he were a neurotic New York drag queen, which everybody agrees sounds wrong coming from a creature that can snap somebody's neck like a brittle twig. "I take revenge for the Hebreweth," he declares in an effete voice, causing his director to fling the teleplay onto the studio floor and storm out, flying into my office to complain. "It's bad enough he lisps out the word 'Hebrews,'" comes the protest, "but he also insists on fluttering his hands around his face like a silent film star and winking at his victims."

Because I created the show and am its executive producer, everybody looks to me for the solution. I have none to offer, and am certain that this is the moment when my fraudulence will become general knowledge. I should not be producing for television.

I have heard that everyone in Hollywood feels like an impostor. But I really am an impostor. My success in this town is based on a short play that I am supposed to have written. Titled *Hard Times on Block A*, the one-act tells the story of a group of prisoners who are planning a riot. They whisper their schemes to each other while tearing off scraps of metal from their beds and sanding them down into makeshift knives. The audience knows these men to be doomed—even Mook, the fresh-faced boy who is struggling to get himself a G.E.D. so that he can get a real job and support his new family once he's out of the pen. When my play debuted at the Western Theater's Festival of New Short Plays, an audience member cried out, "No, Mook— you've got your whole life ahead of you!" This audience member wept openly at the play's climax when a prison guard cornered the boy and beat him to death with a nightstick. The anguished audience member was none other than Whoopie Goldberg, and by the next afternoon I had an agent at William Morris and a meeting at Fox Television.

But I hadn't written *Hard Times on Block A.* I discovered the manuscript in a dumpster outside the California State Prison in Lancaster, which I was digging through in hopes of finding a sandwich. The true author is a convicted spree-killer named Frankie Whitmore, who is called "The Pick-Axe Psycho" by everybody who knows of his heinous mass murders. I receive letters from Whitmore on a daily basis, sometimes several letters per day, all spelling out in graphic detail what Whitmore will do to me when he is paroled. Usually his plans involve duct tape, a sharpened pickaxe, a shallow grave, and a bottle of hydrochloric acid. Fortunately, Whitmore is serving twenty-seven consecutive life sentences, which means he will not be up for parole until he is eighty-six years old. Unless there is a jailbreak, or Whitmore proves to be an uncannily vicious old man, I should be safe.

Nonetheless, his letters terrify me, and I tend to flip through them obsessively as I sit behind my desk at the studio. Although Whitmore has repeatedly gone to the press with his assertion that I stole his play, his accusations have fallen on deaf ears. The fact that he was captured by the FBI while cooking his last victim into a thick, greasy gumbo has encouraged the press into believing that anything Whitmore says is probably crazy. Besides, how could there be anything to the man's claims when I am in the process of developing my own sitcom at Fox Television?

But the television show is also a forgery. Despite having spent the entire previous afternoon digging through dumpsters outside of penitentiaries and county jails, I had no ideas at all when I went in to the Fox Television headquarters at Studio City. I met with Moshe Greenberg, an Orthodox Jewish man who was the executive producer in charge of development. As I entered his office, I found him seated behind his long oaken desk, reading a book. He glanced up at me and then rose to shake my hand. "Mr. Sparber," he said. "Whoopie told me that you write the best dialogue since Mamet! I hope we can find a place for you at Fox."

I thanked him, feeling beads of sweat forming on my forehead. We stood in silence for a few moments, and then my eyes settled on his book. I pointed and shrieked at him, crying out, "What is that?"

"It's a book on Rabbi Judah Loew," Greenberg answered, frowning. "He was a mystic in Sixteenth Century Prague who is supposed to have built a man out of clay to protect the Jewish community from attack. This creature was called a golem."

"How funny," I said. "That's exactly the idea I had for a sitcom."

Greenberg pressed a finger to his lips, intrigued. He sat down, leaned forward towards me, placing his elbows onto the oaken surface of his desk and rested his chin on his hands. "Tell me more," he said.

"Our story is set in contemporary New Jersey," I fibbed, speaking quickly. "A young rabbi named Michael Loew gets a package: a large shipping crate from Prague. He opens it, and discovers a man made from earth. He tries to put the creature to work at his synagogue, but it turns out to have a tendency to go berserk without warning and strangle Gentiles. Hijinks ensue."

"I like it," Greenberg said. "Can we give him a young wife and a nosy next door neighbor?"

"We can give him as many nosy next door neighbors as we want." I declared. "The mud creature can kill a new one every week!"

Greenberg nodded, excited. "But what will we call it?" he asked.

I thought for a moment, and then shrugged. "How about *My Best Friend is a Golem?*"

Greenberg clapped his hands together and nodded. By the beginning of the next week I had my own office at Fox and a team of comedy writers working twelve-hour days to produce fourteen half-hour scripts—an entire season. The writers pestered me constantly with questions, but they required only a "yes" or a "no" from me. I randomly began to agree to some ideas and disagree with others, and despite my nervousness, nobody seemed to notice that my decisions were entirely arbitrary.

"Can we give Rabbi Loew a young daughter?" a writer asked.

"Well, no. No, we can't," I answered, my cheeks heating up. The writer stared at me for a minute with a quizzical expression on his face, and I expected him to point his finger at me and call out "Imposter!" Instead the writer simply nodded, saying, "You're right. The rabbi is too young to have kids."

But the next day another writer asked if we could do an episode in which the Rabbi discovers an underground city buried in his backyard, and I nodded my head eagerly, saying, "That's a swell idea. Keep them coming!" In my erratic universe, a rabbi could not teach inner-city kids the value of sharing, but he could suddenly invent a potion that changed unsuspecting coworkers' genders (in an episode titled *Which Miss is This?*)

In fact, up until we actually began filming, I was starting to feel comfortable in my dual position as the show's chief writer and head honcho. I was surrounded by professionals, many of whom did jobs that I could never hope to fathom (Key grip? Best boy?), and they did them with a cheerful alacrity that lulled me into believing that I could hide my incompetence forever. I would make my fortune in television, and nobody would ever know that I spent my days hiding in my office, browsing through bondage-themed chat rooms on my computer or vainly trying to feed the remains of my Happy Meal lunch to the songbirds that perched outside my window.

But this problem with the actor was going to blow it all. I couldn't solve the problem. Hell, I was afraid of actors. They were often much taller than me and spoke much too loudly. When I met the cast of *My Best Friend is a Golem* at the first script read-through, they hugged me forcefully and boomed about how thrilled they were to be working on such a marvelous comedy, and I spent the remainder of the day hiding in a bathroom. Even the actresses scared me. One of them somehow got hold of my home number and called me, asking questions about her character that I could not possibly answer. "According to the script, Gigi is an *au pair* girl with psychic powers," she said. "How did that affect her when she was a little girl?"

"I can't discuss it right now," I answered in a panic. "The man just came to build the pool."

"Can we get together to talk about it?" she insisted, "perhaps over quiet drinks at my house?"

"I'll call you back and let you know," I cried out, and then hung up the telephone. I quickly picked up the receiver and dialed my phone company to tell them that I needed a new, unlisted telephone number as soon as possible. Then I called a construction company and asked how soon they could come over and build a swimming pool. I spent the next several weeks pretending I had laryngitis, and whenever the actress came to me with questions I simply pointed to my throat and made horrific coughing noises. This trick worked with all the actors, up until this afternoon.

Now, with the show's director opposite me, I briefly consider feigning laryngitis again, but it is too late—he has already heard me speaking, as I have been repeatedly saying, "Sure, the actor playing the golem is a problem, but what do you expect me to do about it?"

"Could you just talk to him?" the director asks. "It's your show, and he respects you. Just tell him that the whole drag queen thing is not such a good idea. I'll call him in, and you speak with him. I'm sure he'll listen to you."

Before I can protest, the director stands and opens my office door. "Big Jim," he calls out, "will you come in here please?" And in walks Big Jim Heywood. He is seven and a half feet tall and thick as a tree trunk. Jim is an ex-wrestler who got his start in film playing villains in Schwartzeneggar movies, and will occasionally relieve stress when he is rehearsing by tearing a telephone book in half. Big Jim is visibly upset. He enters the office and immediately begins pacing, clenching and unclenching his meaty fists. He looks at me, furious, and I glance away from him, pretending to study a letter on my desk.

Unfortunately, I find myself reading one of Frankie Whitmore's vivid descriptions of his plans to disembowel me.

"Everybody agrees, Big Jim," the director says. "It's not working."

Big Jim smashes one fist into a nearby wall with a shout of rage. "Not working?" he cries out. "Screw not working! I'm trying to give my character depth!"

The director shakes his head and puffs out his cheeks, expelling air. "I can't talk to him," he says, throwing his hands up and turning to me. "You talk to him."

Big Jim turns to me as well, eyebrows knitted, lower lip extended into a pout that would be comical on any other man. "You got something to say to me?" Jim asks.

I look down at the letter again, and a line from it catches my eye. "This is my story," I read.

"I know it's your story," Big Jim protests.

"You're stealing my story," I read. Big Jim grows quiet, and then he lowers his head. Encouraged, I read further. "Mess with my story, and you mess with me," I read. "Mess with me, and I start thinking about evil things I might like to do."

"Aw, boss..." Big Jim says, shifting his weight and kicking the ground.

I raise my voice. "I gots all sorts of evil thoughts in my head," I say. "Maybe I'll just get my pick-axe. Maybe I'll drive it so deep into your brain that it explodes out from under your jaw. Maybe I'll tilt you over and let the contents of your skull slide out onto a hot griddle and I'll cook me up a little snack."

"Aw, geez, boss, you don't need to do that," Big Jim says nervously.

"Maybe I'll cook me up a big mess of brains," I cry out, slamming my hand down on my desk. Big Jim flinches. "Maybe I'll spend my afternoon dining on the insides of your empty head! How does that sound?"

Big Jim's mouth drops. He works his jaw a few times, and then holds his hands up protectively. "Whatever you say, boss," he whispers. "I won't mess with your script. I'll read it just like the director says." Then Big Jim turns and flees out the door.

As soon as he is gone, the director guffaws. "That's the way to do it," he says, delighted. "You sure have a way with actors. You're going to go far in this business." He winks at me and exits as my assistant enters, carrying today's batch of mail.

On top of the stack is another letter from Whitman. I tear it open and devour it, looking for paragraphs, sentences, even single words that might come in handy in the future. Maybe later today I will call Whitman and tape-record our conversation. That man has a gift for effective language.

PATHOLOGY

Nonnie Augustine

Nonnie Augustine

How awful it is to dissect a marriage!
We believe it has life, yet we lay it naked
on the therapist's neutral table.
He makes his first incision
into the bloated stomach
of our malnourished union.
He peers inside, trying to see
the hidden workings we've covered
with the taut stretched skin of our collusion.

We pay him to do this!
He hums as he examines,
exposes, probes, takes notes.
He frowns as he checks the damage done
by our withholding of minerals,
protein, fiber.

But we took our marriage to England!
to Ireland! To the Alps!
Once plump and thriving, we never meant
it to become so emaciated and weak.
We may have neglected feedings of late.
We've been tied up elsewhere.
What will you do, Doctor?
Will you prescribe an elixir, painkillers,
a weekend out of town?

TWO POEMS

Truth Thomas

Naptural

Conk my soul CJ—
lie or no lye
iron me dark & lovely.

Fry my esteem CJ.
Burn my neck 100 years long.
Madame, relax me.

I will still be tense
I will still be
fake.

I will always go back
to Africa.

On Mad Cows & Vegetarianism
(4BONIFIDEROJAS)

I've never seen tofu get upset—
not even once.

MY FATHER'S DAUGHTER

Shannon Quinn

want to believe that there is a calculable weight to our memories—that once memories have been removed—the spirit is lighter, free to wander and make associations in any way. I'm trying to convince myself of this as I pace back and forth across my old bedroom floor. This was my bedroom for eighteen years. A lot of my old junk is here. On the shelf is a cheerleading trophy, along with a collection of Judy Blume books and a cheap snow globe that someone must have given me as a present for my high school graduation. Inside it is a mouse in a cap and gown, holding a diploma. Glittering snow confetti rains on his head when I shake it.

I'm hiding in this room. I'm hiding from my father. He doesn't know who I am anymore. He has Alzheimer's. He has always been an extremely logical man. If he could articulate it, he would ask me what my role is, what is my function here? Questions I have been asking myself for most of my life.

Ideas and thoughts sputter, bump and trip out of his mouth. He sings Irish ditties I've never heard before. They are simple and he sings them in full voice and they bother me. They bother me because I don't know them or even the man who is singing them.

My sister says they shouldn't bother me, that he is happy when he is singing. And she's right. He does sound happy when he sings. This discomfort is mine, not his.

He's not singing right now.

He's sitting in his easy chair as if he's waiting for something, but it's like he can never quite manage to figure out what it is. I don't want to go upstairs. I feel small. I'm thirty-three but in my parents' house it seems that I am never more than twelve years old.

Yesterday we went to my niece's wedding. I don't feel old enough to have a married niece.

I dust off the old snow globe and give it a good shake. I watch as the snow swirls around the mouse. In real life, each snowflake is unique—one of a kind—just like our memories. I didn't anticipate that my father's memories, like real life snow, would eventually dissolve, each one lost forever. An empty snow globe is calm, but not very interesting.

Just over three years ago I was sitting on a couch facing a therapist. She looked at me pointedly and said, "Listen, you're working with a limited time budget here, that's why I'm pushing you, you're going to lose the chance to know him." She was right. I did lose the chance to know who my father was. I am called my father's daughter. My mother has always said I am the child most like my father. The problem is I don't know what that means. I try to make myself feel better by thinking it was probably too late to have known him on any other level. That maybe there were no other levels. Maybe he was a simple quiet man. How do you ask a man to define himself, to explain who he is...and quickly, because he's going to forget? Let me know you before you are unknowable.

My father and I are both quiet. We both like books. We don't like crowds. When I was little I would sit on his lap and brush his hair, trying to cover the bald spot on his head. That's where I felt safe. There are other memories of him that come to me when I sit still enough for them to catch up. When I was thirteen years old he brought me a bouquet of yellow roses. I had just won a cheerleading competition. Those yellow roses made me feel like a princess. I remember studying diligently so that when I graduated I would be an Ontario Scholar and he would be proud of me. It feels awkward and strange that I need to excavate my own memories in my search to know him.

I wonder if he is lonely or scared, but can't bring myself to ask, for fear of the answer. We are a family of silence, especially when we hurt. Stoicism has always been my father's way. He takes comfort in my mother. He still knows who she is. She is the woman he has been married to for over fifty-one years and whom he adores.

It's time for me to leave, to go back to my own home. In leaving this house

I want to leave behind the ache that haunts the pit of my stomach and the center of my chest. The whole soft sloppy middle of me hurts. My father is resting in his easy chair. I watch him as he dozes. He is frail and pale. I think about how if he knew me now, as his old cognizant self, he would not have liked or understood some of the choices I have made in my life. Some of my choices would have hurt him, but he wouldn't have stopped loving me and he hasn't stopped loving me—even now, as I kiss his forehead he smiles at me.

His arms reach up to hold me. His grip is still firm and as he holds me, I remember that I am his daughter, whether he knows it or not.

THE WANT ADS

Britni Jackson

1.

wanted: freedom to do pleasing
belly laughs midnight with my beloved
a Triple5soul hoodie in blueberry fuchsia
parents
together
happy brothers granddaddy live
2 bill in the bank of black unity
mi nombre en sus libros
my name in your books

2.

wanted: a president who thinks
change is not a campaign slogan
a country that does not believe in red
and blue segregated to its shores
i need a president to speak in lyric
and rhyme when he walks
maybe then i'll trust the words
that break bread with broken promises

3.

wanted: a suicide song
balmy and deliberate cobalt
lullaby conjuring the goddess
of depression and its amazing
Sade is still alive

4.

wanted: my own car on the A bathed

in patchouli, august beauties and

Gen's sweet potato pie where

bums and street *liberachis* need not apply when

my train runs express

even when the sun heads down to Selene's juke for

a little Shiraz and blue conversation

THE MUTILATED WOMAN

Cathleen Richardson Bailey

Cathleen Richardson Bailey

Love never loses its way home.

Ghanaian Adinkra Symbol & Proverb

❖ ❖ ❖

ong ago, before the organization of time, every village and hamlet kept its own measure, its own record of moments. Claysville, a farming community, moved slowly and based upon their moments, decided things telepathically, by osmosis.

Men and male children talked of land share and expansion, new structures, and preservation of family names. They rose before cocks crowed and sharpened tools to an unmerciful edge, anxious for swift dropping of trees and the touch of good, black earth. They smelled of man, father, brother sweat—pungent, decent, sensual.

Women and female children fried bacon, rolled biscuit dough, and stirred chicken gravy from last evening's meal. They daydreamed of roots: thick, snarled ones to make medicine, do root work, and fashion colors for cloth—burdock root, tree bark. They smelled of hay and warm teats of cows.

Claysville's osmotic tendencies showed prominently in the reproduction of the population. With a collective sigh, children happened in waves, necessities, these familial field hands, only to mature too quickly. Specific times of couplings matured the children—first hand knowledge, nature's window into intimacies, their responsibility to handle, watch, know those times of seasons when new chicks came, and ponies and calves. They performed the all-night vigils in barns, assisting, bloody hands, afterbirth. Maturity came about here too—fickle land, nature's whims, threatened crops. The rough and cracked hands of children helped save fragile roots. Their hearts mourned the dead or dying family dreams.

Mothers wept as daughters neared fifteen. Although matured in land and animal matters, most daughters trembled innocence and naiveté in matters of the heart. Yet in this time, a mother's way dictated encouragement—first dates while she nimbly flashed fingers across quilt frames and embroidery hoops, packed away curtains and starter dishes.

"Is his family prosperous?" mothers asked.

Even the mutilated woman had once been a girl.

Nine years past, the mutilated woman lived with Claysville, eager to give love and receive it. She had wide, innocent eyes and her heart fluttered on Shang—impending wonderment; husband and children; the smell of her own hay and frying bacon; her own snarled roots to uncover; the honest, decent smell of a husband's sweat.

Her mother, Sis, as was her responsibility, asked, "Is his family prosperous?"

The mutilated woman response, "I think so," was enough and Sis said, "Invite Shang Harris to dinner."

Shang appeared, dashing; he dressed in homespun trousers, yes, but the straightness of the lines in them spoke of kings and sophistication. He placed his axe on the doorstep. He whispered, "Hello, it is an honor to grace your table, ma'am," to Sis. And she ushered him into the big room, sparse, but filled with things necessary to accommodate farm people and their needs. One wooden table in the middle was both meeting and dining place. To the right, fading quilts hung from rafters and served as dividers for bedrooms. To the left, a fireplace and cooking stove stood with cords of wood stacked by its side. A smaller room, just at the left of that functioned as pantry for food staples and cooking pots.

A.J. entered, just come in from his field to meet the man come to take his daughter. He spoke softly; yet authoritatively, "Greetings young man."

"It's my pleasure, sir," Shang answered.

"Your axe out front?"

"That it is, sir."

Sis and her daughter hung back to make room for the man-stuff happening in front of them. Years later, Sis remembered being "dry mouthed" and "feeling faint." She took her daughter's hand and they waited for A.J. to wash and join them. A.J. took his time. Shang sat alone at the table while Sis and daughter held hands in front of the piled up cords of wood. They listened to A.J.'s soft whistled song. He splashed water on his face and hands. He could have changed clothes; Sis left his laundered trousers across the bed. But A.J. decided to meet Shang dressed in the dirt of his fields.

At last, A.J. appeared. He motioned for his daughter to seat herself across from Shang. Sis brought in food—roasted yam and corn, warm bread, and sweet red apples. A.J. served and the men talked of prospects, future building, and clearing. The women, though silent, thought of children and hope chests and promises.

Bam! Iron clanged onto the ground in front of A.J.'s house. "That'll be Ogden," he said, "returning my tools." A.J. turned to Shang, "Ogden fixes iron, steady hands, strong."

Shang met A.J.'s eyes. "I've heard as much, sir." He respected A.J., just wouldn't back down. Such is the way with nascent kings, dashing, immature royalty.

A.J. nodded to Sis and she opened the door.

"I won't come inside," Ogden said to Sis, looking in at the daughter. "I see you have company. I'll just put these tools in your shed. They're all, all of them fixed and in good working order."

Ogden turned his glance to Shang. "Evening Shang."

"Evening," Shang replied.

But that was nine years past. The mutilated woman makes her home now on the edge of Claysville's wheat field, in a house honed of thick wood and protected by kudzu vines. Coarse, thick, refined hair covers her head and long breasts hang from her body. She grows round juicy grapes and makes bitter spirits from kudzu leaves. She wears cloth to hide her mutilation; pink cloth left by Claysville women in thanks.

Love gone wild leads to trust and a leaving of our innate senses; a trick the mind plays to force us into focus...or doom. Loradine Stover's eyes settled down comfortably into deceit. When confronted with innocence, Loradine's eyes narrowed and she looked at innocence hard without appearing to do so. The mutilated woman desired Shang Harris, his passion, elegance, and future. Loradine, (Shang's secret woman), studied this desire, this young girl's yearning, this pumping heart, those innocent eyes, that smile.

Loradine befriended the mutilated woman, sat beside her in church, invited her to join the planning committee for the Claysville County Fair, walked with her on market day. She knew how to pry without letting on her intentions and the mutilated woman responded with friendship and an openness that made Loradine laugh out loud, in the evening, when she thought of it, as she sat on the small stool and pressed her face against the smooth skin of the family's cow.

"I think he likes me," the mutilated woman confided in Loradine. "Distant sometimes, as if he loves another. I'll wait though, I'll wait for Shang."

"Do something wild," Loradine suggested, "to get his attention. Give Shang something of yourself, from your body. Make a sacrifice. To bind him to you forever. He'll love you finally. I'm sure of it."

Shang, tender and reckless in the same breath, promised the mutilated woman a tryst in the dark sweet enclave of her father's barn, a romantic interlude, a wisp of a promise at love. She laid herself down, a self-imposed victim, and sliced her left ear, left it dangling just over the edge of the hayloft, her blood dripped all around. Positioned for pity she thought, *He'll love me now.*

Shang smelled injury. He recoiled, reacted to the sight, the torment in her eyes. He loathed self-pity. Shang dropped his axe, anticipated the explosion from its weight, wanted the loud noise to interrupt the circus. He never asked her what happened or why. And in his haste to escape, left his axe behind.

Some, like the mutilated woman, emerge after battle victorious; scars a testament, anxious for new challenges. She didn't tell Sis, wouldn't tell A.J., and left Claysville carrying the knife still covered in blood. She wrapped her head in cloth and tied her ear to the hem of her skirt. In her other hand she carried Shang's axe. She stopped to talk with Ogden.

"You leaving?" he asked.

"Yes."

"A.J. know?"

"Not yet."

"Sis?" And when she didn't answer, Ogden said, "It'll break her heart. Take these," he said handing her his machete and gun, "you'll need them."

She lifted Ogden's machete, draped his gun over her shoulder and walked through the wheat field away from Claysville. On the other side, she found a clearing just under a stand of trees, beside a gentle brook.

She buried her ear and the knife where her grape vines flourish now. She placed Ogden's machete on the ground to mark a spot for shelter. She used Shang's axe to chop wood for her house. With each felled tree, tears. In this way, she repaired herself and understood mutilation as an outward manifestation of this lie—insecurity. She smiled, felt honorable, and new blood coursed. How thick and sweet and strong. She wondered, *What will be my work?*

Sweat poured, she put her lips to the brook and drank long. She toiled all the days and well into the nights, never questioning her strength, just marveling at it. For nine days she cut and carried and positioned wood. At the end of a day her strength waned. The dark sky transmitted instructions: *Not inside yet,* it said, and she laid herself upon the ground. The moon and stars bathed her and she awoke restored.

Once during the noonday sun, she looked up to question its intensity and all at once, felt Shang's presence. She looked in the direction of the pull. He had come in search of his axe and unable to face her, stood just at the edge of the wheat field closest to Claysville. He seemed so small and her muscles rippled as she pulled on and directed the heft of the great axe.

A day came for completion. She stood back to behold her house, heaved the axe into the wheat field, and opened her door. Sometimes she can still see the axe, the blade rusting and glinting in the moonlight.

Kudzu came and taught her how to brew its leaves into bitter spirits; the drink sustained her strength. Wild grapes came and she made jam and sweet wine from peelings. Wild pigs appeared when she was hungry. She aimed Ogden's gun and with one bullet, salivated about fresh bacon. She built herself a smokehouse. From pig fat she made soap, and boiling some of the other fat down with water from her brook and juice from her grapes and scents from lavender and chamomile growing nearby, she made salve for her hands and feet and sweet oil for her hair.

She claimed a patch of Claysville's wheat field. No one questioned the mutilated woman; instead built fences around theirs and left her chosen patch open and free. From this small plot she cultivated wheat for bread and biscuits and crust for apple pies.

Sheep came and she spun their wool and wove it into cloth. In the morning, songbirds weighed down trees' branches and she had music. At night, wolves howled and she was comforted. Soon her schedule of moments aligned themselves into days and weeks and months. She went about her organized increments of time, singing at first light, spinning, putting up jam, frying bacon, sewing, and drinking her peeling wine and bitter brew. The mutilated woman looked skyward and then toward Claysville. She was expecting a new thing from the sky and uninvited guests from Claysville.

One night the stars lowered and threw bold illumination into her house. She unwrapped her hair, exposed her mutilation, and laid herself down on the ground.

"On this night you will sleep with us," the heavens said. "Dream of new life. Giving. That will be your life's work."

The mutilated woman slept before God, the moon bathed her and stars twinkled over her body. She was not afraid and her spirit journeyed into the realm of the unfathomable. She understood all things.

In the morning, the singing birds welcomed her return. She slid her body into the brook's cool water. She shivered but accepted its gentle current. She moved with it and remembering last night's spirit journey, touched her belly, thought of her womb; was overcome with happiness and then grief. She remembered the prophecy, the loss.

For the next nine months, she carried the Star Child. She took long walks into the forest. Large sticks presented themselves to her for assistance when, after a time, her body grew thick and cumbersome with child. She thought of strawberries and new crops sprouted. She longed for cow's milk and followed the sound of a deep, clanging bell. She drank warm, fresh milk, swallowing its bits of fat. After a time, she churned butter and waited to cut thick slices of cheese.

Soon the full moon moved above her house and she squatted on the ground to push and strain and labor. The Star Child plopped down, fat and warm and slippery; dark as night with wide innocent eyes and a birthmark on the back of her hand in the shape of the fat from the cow's milk.

"Willful," the mutilated woman spoke to the Star Child, "that's what you'll be."

The Star Child smiled to songbirds in the morning and lay on blankets during the day to watch work—spinning, churning, weaving, baking. The Star Child *was* willful and tentative steps evolved into adventure, always into the wheat fields and towards Claysville beyond.

"Where are you, baby?" the mutilated woman asked, searching by the brook and in the wheat field. "Come," she soothed when finding her, "stay with mother." She removed leaves from kudzu vines; wove the vines into a long, strong rope; tied one end to the Star Child's ankle and tied the other end to her own.

One day the sky opened and torrential rain fell hard upon the earth. The mutilated woman hurried with the Star Child into the safety of her house. She sat at the window and watched the hard rain trample the wheat fields and harass the grape vines and shake the roof of the smokehouse. The kudzu trembled and banged against the roof, leaves flew everywhere. Angry ripples appeared in the brook and it rushed downward, irritated and annoyed. Thunder boomed across the sky and lightening snaked out hissing and retreating. Thunder thrilled the Star Child; she giggled and clapped her hands.

The sun burst open and brought with it light and warmth and transformation. The mutilated woman surveyed the damage to her wheat field and grape vines and noticed the men of Claysville taking stock of their own. Two people emerged through the wheat field's devastation. She fought against the inevitable and snatched up the Star Child. She held her close and kissed her eyes and cheeks and hands. The Star Child gazed into the eyes of the approaching couple, Shang Harris and Loradine Stover.

The mutilated woman touched her scar but felt no emotional attachment to it or her long ago behavior. She did remember her action; however, and instead of shame, felt the honor of her own blood running through her veins thick and sweet and strong. She cupped her hands and caught liquid from her breasts and smiled about new life. She marveled at her strength. She glanced at Shang's great axe still rusting in the wheat field. She thought of peeling wine, headcheese, biscuits, and lavender salve. All these things.

By the time Shang and Loradine reached her, she was holding the Star Child and standing by a tree stump, the blade of Ogden's machete stuck in, her scar wrapped in beautiful cloth.

"I couldn't stop her," Shang said pointing to Loradine. "She was struck dumb, not long after you left. Ain't been able to utter one word. Last thing she said had to do with dreams and babies, a mark on a tiny hand like fat floating in fresh milk. Loradine got a powerful hurt, a woman hurt down there. Can't have no babies. Then today after the thunder, she grabbed my hand hard and we commenced running this way."

The mutilated woman took a deep breath and blew into the Star Child's ear. "Loradine must ask. That's the only way."

"Loradine can't talk," Shang began, but Loradine interrupted, "She's mine, give her to me."

"No Loradine," the mutilated woman said. "You must ask me. That's the only way."

So Loradine kneeled. "Please," she asked so gently. "Please. I lived with your shame and this baby in my head for nine years. Couldn't speak. I knew she was dark as night. I knew she had eyes somebody could fall into. I knew about the shape like milk fat." Loradine stretched her shaking hands. "Please. May I have her?"

Hard work and generous gifts from God began the transformation. Her new thing.

Shang and Loradine began the uninvited guests. Her giving.

The Star Child giggled and clapped her hands.

The mutilated woman suffered at first, the house so empty and calm. Yet, based upon her healed spirit, she understood that like Shang's love, what wasn't hers wasn't hers, even if she helped create it.

Other uninvited guests came in the still of the evening. People needing answers and confirmation. Women with dry breasts and men not able to satisfy. People seeking good graces and others, seeking retribution.

On retribution, the mutilated woman offered bitter spirits, "Taste bitter," she'd say and offer the cup. "Retribution belongs to God alone. Go away, I can't help you." And always in a few days the ones seeking retribution returned with bowed heads, "What is it I must do?"

The mutilated woman asked nothing of her guests but the burden of her good graces obligated the faithful to leave gifts. She found them on and around the grape vines; money wrapped in pink fabric, white goats, hens.

Time passed. The stars illuminated her house. She slept on the ground and her spirit journeyed into the realm of the unfathomable. The next morning, song-birds welcomed her return. She picked up Ogden's machete and, following instructions, walked parallel to the gentle brook. She swung his machete and carved a new path. At the end of it, she saw a little stone house with smoke jutting up from a crooked chimney. Yellow flowers bloomed below the windows. Moss from the brook grew up out of the water and prepared a perfect path to its door. Another structure, a lean-to with tools and fire and anvil sat nearby.

The mutilated woman paused and then lowered herself into the stream. *Tomorrow I'll bathe in my tub, rub on sweet oil, and put on a new dress,* she thought watching the chimney's smoke, *and then I'll come back.*

Ogden stood back from his window, he watched her, expectant, never giving up on the divine; the thing God wrote about in heaven. Tomorrow he'd meet her half way.

She walked toward Ogden. He smiled when he saw her. She noticed his straight white teeth.

"Oralee," Ogden said extending his hands, sturdy with dirt under his fingernails. He came shirtless with a red cloth tied around his forehead. He noticed her bare feet, the hem of her skirt dancing in the breeze and that her white hair, uncovered, nappy, and pulled back, revealed her mutilation like a dare.

"Ogden," the mutilated woman observed, "you call me by my name."

"Sis is dead," Ogden said, "and A.J.'s an old man."

"Pity about Sis," Oralee said. "Maybe I'll visit A.J. Take him healing salve, rub his old feet."

"He'd like that," Ogden said. "He'd like that just fine."

Seasons passed. Ogden manipulated fire and iron, respected it and loved Oralee. She welcomed uninvited guests, gave love, received it, and cherished Ogden's commitment to possibilities. They worked hard and grew fat and rich upon the land, the generous gift from God. On a certain week they lived together in the stone house with the crooked chimney. On another week they lived in the house honed of thick wood and covered in kudzu.

There was another thing…a sometimes occurrence nine years forward that happened at night just under the full moon when Oralee and Ogden sat together outside. Deep set, round, sparkling eyes peeked out at them through the wheat field.

"Wondering eyes," Ogden said.

"Yes," Oralee answered with a smile. "Watching eyes. Considering eyes. Love eyes. Willful."

THREE POEMS

Diana Marie Delgado

Diana Marie Delgado

Natural History

Autumn was sweet, you called.
We sat at the end of the bed and pulled off
my clothes. The dollar was strong and scientists
created an igloo for a man who'd been dead
over ten thousand years. His last meal was acorn
and venison. Autumn was kind, she had gone.
I didn't leave the house and practiced sleeping.
The beating of a man was caught on the black
tongue of a videotape, and a lizard was found
curled inside an egg like an eyelash. It was said
to be the most ancient unborn fossil ever.
Autumn was sweet, was it not? We argued
about God. He should kill everything
and start over. I believed. You did not.

Man Of The House

My brother sleeps in the living room.
I live in the kitchen.
The eaves are empty of bees.

I'm on my stomach, reading.
My brother rolls a rifle in carpet.
Prove that I'm overreacting I yell.

And wash your hands with soap.
I can smell your cigarette way over here.
He's brought home diamonds.

Mother scratches them
against the coffee table glass.
The birds argue in the elms.

Father sulks. *Who does he think he is*
bringing home such finery?

Twelve Trees

The plumes of the avocado are sick.
Dad cuts roses with a hatchet.
Beetles swarm the figs. Crystals form in the honey.
In hell there's nothing but crocodiles
and fathers. In Mexico the devil is handsome
and is caught smiling in all his photographs.
He has one wife, and two daughters, three sons,
but no father. He rakes leaves and fixes
umbrellas, tends twelve trees, and occasionally
throws back his head and sings.

AN INTERVIEW WITH
NICHOLAS MONTEMARANO

Jasai Madden

When Nicholas Montemarano wrote his debut Novel, *A Fine Place* he managed to cover a human perspective that in all of my years of reading, I had never considered. As I watched the daily lives of the family members of a convicted murder accomplice, I began to see with harsh clarity the community and circumstance that comprise the "other" side of a terrible tragedy. When the victims of a crime have had their say and shouted through their tears, what is in the heavy hearts of, and on the frantic minds of the perpetrator and their family? At first I cringed at the idea that for them— grandmothers, grandfathers, aunts, and childhood friends—there is love and understanding, sympathy and hope for a perpetrator's tomorrows, but then I read Nicholas' story. What I discovered between the pages of *A Fine Place* is that all people are fragile and nuanced. Whether or not they fall on the appropriate side of our own moral fence, there is a story to be told about why and how they began on the road that became their life's journey. Nicholas's telling of the lives of these characters that are so held together and at the same time so heavily burdened by the love they endure for a young son involved in a terrible crime, left me feeling both awful and enlightened.

JASAI MADDEN: *Of all the stories that shuffle around in your subconscious begging to be explored through your writing—and from reading some of your short stories I can tell that the range of ideas, topics, and even writing styles that you employ are widely various—what was it about the subject matter that is the framework for* A Fine Place, *that caused you to write at such length? Especially considering that in the real scenario that this fictional account is taken from, the "Tony" character—who you are related to in some way—was, to my understanding, acquitted of any wrongdoing?*

NICHOLAS MONTEMARANO: Everything I write comes directly from my life. This doesn't mean that everything I write is strictly autobiographical, but rather that my stories grow out of whatever concerns are pressing on me at any given moment. I can chart my life, my biography, through my stories. At the time I started writing *A Fine Place,* some of my older relatives were dying, and I knew they were taking a lot of secrets to the grave, most importantly the story—or their version of it—of the racially-motivated murder of Yusuf Hawkins in Brooklyn in 1989. My cousin went on trial for murder—he was one of a group of white kids there when Hawkins was shot—but he was acquitted. He later went to prison for something unrelated. My extended family was always very secretive about the whole thing, and I was intrigued by their silence about something so huge, so I started to write about it. I chose fiction because it gives me the most freedom—I'm not wedded to any facts, and that's the way I like it. I chose a novel, rather than a short story, because this particular story needed to be told from multiple points of view—it simply couldn't be contained in twenty or thirty pages. Once the story became fiction, what happened in real life no longer mattered; the only thing that mattered, at that point, was that I write a good story.

JASAI MADDEN: *Why write from the seemingly second-hand perspective of the grandparents and great aunt? Characters that, in the real situation, would have been thought of as peripheral to the event that took place?*

NICHOLAS MONTEMARANO: I wanted Tony to be a bit of a mystery and the murder to be way in the background. This is why the novel includes only a few pages about the murder—the first short chapter and parts of the final chapter. The rest would be about how the murder and Tony's imprisonment affected the rest of the family. I'd initially planned to write the novel without a single appearance by Tony—we'd hear only from his older relatives—but I quickly discovered that I needed Tony, too. Still, most readers tell me that the story belongs to the older characters, not Tony. I think I agree with them.

JASAI MADDEN: *You said that stories grow out of whatever concerns are pressing you at any given moment, that one could chart your life through your stories. Are there any subjects that, for some reason, you have been reluctant to write about? And if so, how do you settle that with your creative self?*

NICHOLAS MONTEMARANO: Not really. If something is pressing on me, I'll try to write about it. I try my best not to keep any secrets from myself. I write about things that bother or move or puzzle me, things I'm afraid of. You have to be willing to write about those things you're most afraid to write about. You have to be willing to turn all your secrets into stories. Otherwise they die with you and you've lost an opportunity to share with others what it means to be human. I've written about some sensitive subjects, and I've certainly written stories that might upset people. The possibility of upsetting people never stops me from writing a story; it might stop me from publishing a story, or from including a story in a book, but it would never stop me from writing it. The subjects that are closest to me usually come out after time has passed, and in subtle but stubbornly consistent ways. I'm not interested in writing stories anyone else can write; my goal is to write stories no one else in the universe can write because they're not me. The best way to do that is to write from your own experience and vision.

JASAI MADDEN: *Do you think that the second life of secrets—that half where the story finally gets told by those who have not necessarily carried the heavy burden of them for so many years—is ever as grave or deteriorating as the holding, the hoarding really, of secrets?*

NICHOLAS MONTEMARANO: Holding on to secrets—especially secrets about yourself—has to be one of the worst burdens. I have a very difficult time doing it. It's probably why I have a small number of very close friends rather than a large number of acquaintances. I'm a fairly quiet person, but if you ask me about myself I'm usually an open book. I don't like small talk very much; I want to know all your secrets, all the real meat of your life. I want to know what you love, what you're afraid of, what crosses you bear, what brings you pain and joy—now that's a conversation I want to be a part of. Same is true with writing: I want to write and read stories that don't pussyfoot around. No small talk. Tell me right away what the wound of the story is. So, to answer your question: I think the telling—the unloading of secrets—is usually liberating, frightening, yes, but ultimately liberating. The burden is not in telling, but in not telling.

JASAI MADDEN: *Sounds like you would be a pretty intense first date—L and J says hello to your lovely wife!—Your sentiments about wanting to know only the truest things about a person's life were very striking. I was startled by the honesty conveyed when you said that you want to know all of the secrets: what someone loves, their pains, and the crosses they bear. I can tell when read-*

ing both the novel and your short stories that you are extremely deft when it comes to taking such admittances and creating characters that embody perfectly, people and circumstances very unlike you or your own. Do you find that as a result, people closest to you are leery or guarded? Afraid that their personality or one of their more noteworthy scenarios might turn up in one of your stories?

NICHOLAS MONTEMARANO: I don't think so. The people I'm closest with understand that I'd never exploit a person or his/her situation; I'd only try to write a moving story that expresses some truth, as I see it, about being alive. For the most part, I think the people in my life appreciate my openness and my desire to truly know them. Writers have a reputation—mostly deserved—for being the literary equivalent of ambulance chasers. I'm thinking of a writer who might jot notes for a story or poem at his own mother's funeral. Some writers never turn off their story radar to stop for a moment and be human. While my story radar is usually on, I'm a human being first, and sometimes I need to turn it off. I trust that the most important things I experience or witness will find their way into my stories just when I need them to, maybe years later.

JASAI MADDEN: *A great deal of time is spent on physicality in this story,* [A Fine Place], *especially as it relates to the struggles associated with the aging of the body and illness. Is there some symbolism that can be attached to this thread of the storyline or is it simply circumstantial and present more as a vehicle for driving the elderly characters that are central to the story?*

NICHOLAS MONTEMARANO: I don't think physical details in a story should be included simply as window dressing. The characters' physical deterioration does symbolize the deterioration of the family unit, their way of life, the neighborhood, etc., but I didn't consciously include those details as symbols; to do so consciously would have been heavy-handed. I included them because when I looked at the older people in my family—the people I saw in my mind as I invented the characters in the novel—I tried to put myself in their shoes, in their bodies, and what I felt more than anything was how the body breaks down, how old age is a series of trips to the doctor, is getting from one room to the other and walking up and down flights of stairs to get the mail. I was twenty-seven when I wrote this novel, and I put my twenty-seven year-old self into the bodies of people who were in their seventies and eighties, so what I felt was: Oh my God, being old isn't easy! How do you get into and out of the tub when you're ninety? To be an effective writer, you have to be empathetic; you have to be able to put yourself into other people's minds and bodies, to feel what they feel.

JASAI MADDEN: *You teach creative writing at Franklin and Marshall College in Pennsylvania—what is the most valuable thing that you hope your students come away with at the end of one of your courses?*

NICHOLAS MONTEMARANO: Certainly you can teach students some of the basics: how to avoid sentimentality without being cold, how to push through the ordinary in order to find something truly original, how to surprise a reader, how to edit sentences, et cetera. But the most important thing I'd want my students to realize is this: If you want to be the best writer you're capable of being, you must be very brave. You must be willing to write the most important thing. As Gordon Lish has said, every story should go like this: "I have to tell you this. Whatever I do, I can't not tell you this." Most students begin by writing stories based on other stories they've read, or based on movies, and I have to say to them, 'If this were the last story you could ever write, would this be the one? If not, go write that story.'

JASAI MADDEN: *Tell us about the place where you write, the physical environment and if you think place is important to the process of good/productive writing.*

NICHOLAS MONTEMARANO: Most often, I write in the morning for a few hours. If a story is going well, I'll write as long as I have to. I used to write every day because I believed that I was supposed to, and that worked for me. But now I don't feel that I have to write every day, especially if I'm between stories. In fact, sometimes it's best to take a day off and let a story or scene gestate. I live in a fourth-floor walk-up in Philadelphia with my wife and dog, so when I'm not teaching I'll usually write by the window at my dead grandfather's rickety old desk, the dog sleeping on the floor next to me. If that's not working, I might write in bed. I never write in public or in a cafe or anything like that—I need quiet. Once a year, I spend a month or so at an artist's colony—usually The MacDowell Colony or Yaddo. This is the best atmosphere for writing—you have a quiet studio, and your meals are prepared for you, and there are other artists in studios nearby for you to have dinner and drinks with. You don't have to do anything but write—no bills to pay, no phones to answer, nothing. It's wonderful. So yes, I do believe the physical environment matters.

JASAI MADDEN: *What is your favorite book? Why?*

NICHOLAS MONTEMARANO: It's difficult to name one. I tend to like short-story collections more than novels. I love Raymond Carver's *Where I'm Calling From* and Virginia Woolf's *To the Lighthouse* and David Means's *Assorted Fire Events* and many of John Edgar Wideman's stories. If I had to name one book, it would be Denis Johnson's *Jesus' Son*, which everyone in the world should read if they haven't. His stories are raw and intense and seem to meander in a kind of reckless way, but deep down, they really are tightly written and risky and utterly unique. The writer who excites me the most right now is Charles D'Ambrosio. His story collection *The Point* is fantastic, and so are his new stories that have appeared in *The New Yorker*—dark and intense and beautifully crafted.

JASAI MADDEN: *Who is your favorite character in a novel or short story? Why?*

NICHOLAS MONTEMARANO: It's so funny, I rarely think in terms of characters. When I read a great Charles D'Ambrosio story, I think of Charles D'Ambrosio, or his sentences, but never his characters. That said, the one character who seems to pop into my head most often is Stevens, the English butler who narrates Kazuo Ishiguro's remarkable novel *The Remains of the Day*. More than any other character, Stevens breaks my heart. He's so painfully repressed, I want to leap into the novel and make him feel.

JASAI MADDEN: *What is you favorite word?*

NICHOLAS MONTEMARANO: I have the word 'Truth' tattooed on my wrist, so I'd say that's an important word to me. Ironic that a fiction writer would have the word 'truth' on his wrist. I don't think I have a favorite word, but I have a favorite sentence. It's from Stanley Elkin's short story "A Poetics for Bullies." It's told from the POV of a bully named Push. The sentence goes: "Push pushed pushes."

JASAI MADDEN: *Give us your best writing tip.*

NICHOLAS MONTEMARANO: Please understand that you are going to write bad stories, but it's okay. You have to write the bad in order to get to the good. This will never change, no matter how good of a writer you become. Don't be ashamed or discouraged by it. Laugh at it. Be grateful for it. Just don't publish any of it! Oh yeah, one more tip: Your first sentence must be amazing; it must be the best sentence you've ever written. Once you've accomplished that, then your second sentence must be the best sentence you've ever written. Lather, rinse, repeat.

JASAI MADDEN: *Is there anything else that you have been just dying to share with readers?*

NICHOLAS MONTEMARANO: Writing is its own reward. Don't worry about being famous. It will only weaken your work.

JASAI MADDEN: *Thank you for you time Nicholas, it has been my pleasure.*

NICHOLAS MONTEMARANO: Thank you—it's been *my* pleasure, really.

CONTRIBUTORS

NONNIE AUGUSTINE on writing *Pathology*

The first line in *Pathology* came to me as my husband and I drove silently home after a marriage counseling session. The couples counselor had used the word *collision* and one thing led to another, as they say. I wrote the first draft of the poem that night. The couples counseling was not going well.

Nonnie Augustine has a B.F.A. in dance from Julliard. A degree which allowed her to both dance professionally and teach dance. She has published poetry online in the e-zine, The Beat *and has had an essay published in the literary magazine,* The Pegasus Review.

CATHLEEN RICHARDSON BAILEY
on writing *The Mutilated Woman*

The Mutilated Woman was inspired by the story of the Yoruba Òrisà, Sàngó and Òbà. In that story, Òbà was betrayed, exiled, and redeemed and is a ultimately about self-examination and triumph over obstacles. *The Mutilated Woman*, although inspired by Òbà, takes on a life of its own. This story taught me a great deal about how to tune the ears, about how to listen to characters and about how to give the characters room so that they can tell their own story. I found listening to and writing this story both challenging and rewarding; a gift from above. *The Mutilated Woman* is taken from a collection of stories titled *The Mutilated Woman and Other Tales.*

Cathleen Richardson Bailey is a self-taught writer and textile artist, a 2003 recipient of Pennsylvania Council on the Arts' Fellowship in Literature, and a 2004 Kimmel Harding Nelson Center for the Arts Fellow. Her stories have appeared in Shooting Star Literary Review, Progress Magazine, Stickman Review *and* Cake Train: A Journal of Writing. *Bailey has shared her gift of combining creative writing and fiber art with various organizations including Brooklyn Public Library, Cuyahoga Valley National Park and The Pennsylvania Council on the Arts Artists-in-Education Residency Program. Further information about this artist can be found at www.cathleenbailey.com*

MARK BUDMAN on writing *A Treatise on the Power of Reading*

A short while back, I saw a car with a vanity license plate at a rest area. It said "Book Fun" or something similar. I thought what kind of person would advertise the love of books to the 21st century world of digital media? While driving home, I tried to reconstruct in my mind this curious personality. That's how *A Treatise on the Power of Reading* was born. One little seed grew into one little story that covered the imaginary person's entire life span.

Mark Budman's fiction and poetry have appeared or are scheduled to appear in Mississippi Review, Virginia Quarterly, Iowa Review, Cafe Irreal, Exquisite Corpse, Web Del Sol, McSweeney's, Conversely *and elsewhere.* Exquisite Corpse *nominated Mark for the XXVI Pushcart Prize. He is the publisher of the flash (short-shorts) fiction magazine* Vestal Review *http://www.vestalreview.net.*

RICK CASTANEDA on writing *Proportions of Boxes: Four Pieces of Sudden Fiction*

This title and all of the stories speak to the cubicle world a lot of the characters are trying to escape, how they're all trying to think 'outside the box,' as well as the world of regulations, proportions, and rules that they all live in and outside of.

Rick Castaneda lives in Los Angeles, a graduate of the Creative Writing Program at the University of Southern California where he studied under T.C. Boyle but he grew tall in Eastern Washington very close to Raymond Carver's old stomping grounds in the Yakima Valley. This is Rick's first published story unless you count student publications and movie reviews. (We do).

DIANA MARIE DELGADO on writing *Twelve Trees*

The impulse for *Twelve Trees* stems from my summers in Mexico, where the devil is said to arrive at dances, impeccably dressed and looking for the souls of "misbehaving" women. This idea of evil in the guise of goodness was of particular interest to me.

Diana Marie Delgado lives in New York City and is finishing her MFA in Poetry at Columbia University. Her poems have appeared in Border Senses, The Laurel Review *and* The North American Review. *She is the author of the chapbook,* Holding Nothing Like It's Something.

PATRICIA GOMES on writing
*For (*insert your name here*), I Did Know You*

The back story of this poem is actually mundane with a hint of nostalgia. While going through old photo albums, reliving my youth, a strip of photo booth pictures fell to the floor. They'd been buried behind an 8 x 10. You guessed it—Mr. Beige himself. I'd forgotten all about him...or maybe I'd just denied his existence. Now, in middle-age, I feel I treated him shabbily and the poem is my (almost!) public apology.

Patricia Gomes is author of the chapbook, Stroking Castro's Beard, *Patricia was named the First Place Winner in iVillage's Annual Poetry Slam in 2002 and 2003. She was awarded second Place in 2004. Included in numerous poetry anthologies, her recent works appear in* Literary Potpourri, Shadow Keep Magazine, *and* Dark Krypt. *Last fall, her short story,* Illegal Aliens *was included in the anthology* Other Worlds: Alien Alerts.

NOAH GROSSMAN on writing *October*

The poem *October* came about after seeing a commercial for a scary movie. I don't like being scared. My roommate loves horror films. Anyway, I thought about the phase "I hate being scared," and the poem plopped out of my clenched, sweaty brain.

Noah Grossman is a young writer living in New York, graduated from Cornell University and currently looking for employment.

DEBBIE ANN ICE on writing *Sculpting*

My stories are pure imagination, sparked by one incident, experience, or brief moment that inspires me, usually while on my morning run, to think through an emotion. The moment that sparked *Sculpting* lasted about one minute, which was how long the skin doctor took to tell me I had melanoma. While the initial diagnosis was wrong, and I am fine, that experience stayed with me. I thought a lot about death's relationship to life and our desperate need to leave an eternal imprint. Other themes and emotions evolved as I wrote and understood the character.

Debbie Ann Ice's work has appeared in 3A.M. *magazine,* Salome *magazine,* Literary Mama, Pindeldyboz, In Posse, Barbaric Yawp, *and others. Her spirit is still sauntering about low country Georgia, where she was born and raised; however, her body now resides in Connecticut, where she lives with her husband, two boys and feisty, fat English bulldog. She misses low country Georgia and writes about that culture occasionally, but only occasionally. She is thrilled to be a part of* Lorraine and James.

BRITNI JACKSON on writing *The Want Ads*

My motivation for *The Want Ads* was originally a writing exercise. The exercise was to write a "want ad" for yourself, which led me to write the first one...which is basically all about what I want in my life. Then I decided to expand upon that and write a few more. The second came directly after the 2004 presidential elections and the last two...just figments of my imagination.

Britni Jackson lives and writes in Brooklyn, New York. She is a founding member of the Silent Fusion Collective and is presently nearing the completion of her MFA in Poetry at Brooklyn College. Britni is also the Poetry Editor for Lorraine and James.

DANIEL JAFFE on writing *Modern Times*

For the past couple of years, I've periodically been writing short stories for *The Forward,* a Jewish newspaper. Each story is designed to illuminate issues from a particular weekly portion of the Hebrew Bible. So, I begin writing the stories with a given set of issues and themes, and then I seek characters whose lives engage with them. When starting *Modern Times,* I focused on the theme of adultery, an issue in the weekly Bible portion, and I added in the theme of hypocritical, self-serving reliance on the Bible, an issue in the world around us.

Daniel Jaffe is the award-winning author of the novel The Limits of Pleasure, *compiler and editor of* With Signs and Wonders: An International Anthology of Jewish Fabulist Fiction, *and translator of the Russian-Israeli novel* Here Comes the Messiah! *by Diana Rubina. His short stories and essays have appeared in dozens of literary journals and anthologies and he contributes fiction regularly to* The Forward. *Dan teaches fiction writing for the UCLA Extension Writers' Program and he is the Consulting Editor for* Lorraine and James.

PAMELA MACISAAC on writing *Sweet Potato and Coconut*

A number of different things came together when I wrote this story, including a very real pair of very noisy children living in the apartment upstairs. Like most of my stories, it flowed from an imagined juxtaposition of character and situation—i.e. a fed-up, overwhelmed academic confronted with an ongoing irritant and his excessive response to said irritant. The rest has no basis in anything except a storytelling impulse.

Pamela MacIsaac has published short fiction and poetry in a variety of journals, including Jones Ave., Another Toronto Quarterly, paperplates, Plum Ruby Review, Transition, *and* Projected Letters. *She lives in Toronto with her always-wonderful partner, continually amazing daughter, and embarrassingly spoiled pets.*

MARCIA LYNX QUALEY on writing *Marked*

Marked started when I pictured a woman waking up with the eye in the center of her palm. The eye seemed both internal and external—her own judgment and society's. After that, I just followed her around.

Marcia Lynx Qualey fled no apparent persecution in the Midwest for a life in the Middle East, where she writes and wrangles a fifteen-month-old boy. Her fiction has appeared recently or is forthcoming in Middle Eastern and North American journals, including Woman This Month *(Bahrain),* Wild Strawberries, Sexy Stranger, Smokelong Quarterly, Lenox Avenue, Pindeldyboz, *and* Flashquake.

SHANNON QUINN on writing *My Father's Daughter*

This piece came out of a series of reflections on my father. In some ways they were motivated by guilt. We live in different cities. In writing this I was trying to accept how much and how little I know of the whole man.

Shannon Quinn lives in Toronto. She has had short fiction published in THIS Magazine *and* Taddle Creek Magazine. *She also writes and produces documentaries for radio.*

HALIMAT SEKULA on writing *Pure Water Girl*

I was inspired to write the *Pure Water Girl* one day in Abuja when I noticed that more than 75% of the child laborers in and around a popular park were girls below sixteen. There was this particular girl who refused to budge even when I refused to buy her ware. Such persistence in one so young touched something in me and I realized that the harsh socio-economic reality of many Nigerian families is taking its toll on young girls and even boys.

Nigerian-born Halimat Sekula lectures in The Department of English, Nasarawa State University Keffi. Her poems and short stories have been published in various anthologies and newspapers such as KUKA: Journal of English Literary Association, Nigerian Newsday, Poetry from A.B.U. *and* Penwomanship. *A collection of her poems titled* Tongues of Flame *has just been published.*

MAX SPARBER on writing *A Gift for Effective Language*

I have been involved with an Omaha theater, the Blue Barn, for years, as an actor and a playwright. They have a longstanding tradition of producing humorous material of questionable taste, and, inevitably, they claim the play in question was stolen from a Dumpster, often outside a prison, and I have often wondered what the results would be if such a claim were true. Additionally, I lived in Hollywood for about four years, attempting to make a go of working as a screenwriter. At parties, people predictably ask each other what their more recent project is, but I was spectacularly unsuccessful as a screenwriter, and so would just invent screenplays on the spot. In one instance, I had Tarzan battling Abraham Lincoln in a script titled "Ape

Lincoln." *My Best Friend is a Golem,* was another ersatz project, in which a young man finds himself in possession of a deadly mystical creature. In this story, I just sort of welded a few of these ideas together as a falsely autobiographical tale featuring myself as the incompetent narrator whose thievery and lack of imagination have allowed him to ascend to great power in Hollywood, which doesn't seem altogether improbable.

Max Sparber is a writer and playwright living in the French Quarter of New Orleans, just around the corner from the site of the J&M Studio, where Roy Brown recorded "Good Rockin' Tonight," Fats Domino recorded "The Fat Man," and Little Richard recorded "The Girl Can't Help It." Sparber's plays include Cruelties, *inspired by the dissolute final years of New Orleans-born writer Truman Capote, and* Minstrel Show, *based on the real-life lynching of an African-American in Omaha in 1919. This is his first published story.*

JESS STUART on writing *Blood of the Lamb*

Well, it came from a sweatshirt of all things! The design on the front was a Christmas motif—the outline of the stable, the manger, a gleaming star overhead; all the traditional figures. But the caption underneath it read "It's a girl!" When I stopped laughing I got to thinking "What if..." and then started writing how I thought this most interesting idea might have played out.

Jess Stuart earned a Masters of Pastoral Ministry in 1997 and has been freelancing for religion and spirituality journals ever since. Her articles have appeared in a number of Canadian and American journals and several Canadian newspapers. Her poetry has been published in Room of One's Own *and* On Spec

Magazine. Her fiction has appeared in Liguorian, Writer On Line, *and* Quantum Muse. *In 2000 she was nominated for a Canadian Church Press Award and she finished second in* Room of One's Own *National Poetry Contest for 2004. She completed a novella in December 2003, and is working on her first full-length novel. Jess lives in a small town in southwestern Ontario, Canada.*

KRISTI SWADLEY on writing
Too Many Saltine Crackers Will Dry Out Your Mouth

The title came to me first. Just popped into my head out of nowhere, but no words followed. So, it lingered in a *Word* document, and a few days later I was thinking about Adam Sandler's character in *Punch Drunk Love,* and the story poured out. The title serves as a metaphor for my character's inability to speak out against the tyrannical people in his life. On one hand it has nothing to do with the story, and on the other, it is the story. Have you ever eaten saltine crackers without a drink? Bit hard to speak, isn't it? I like titles that make people think and, obviously, this one succeeded in doing just that. The story just wrote itself. I didn't really have time to think about it, it just had to be written. I write what I see in my head and I often don't have any clue how it will turn out. In this case, the poem turned out far better that I ever dared to hope. It has become one of my personal favorites.

Kristi Swadley is an assistant editor for Lily: A Monthly Online Literary Review. *She lives and breathes with her family in a Midwestern town and writes in a world of her own. Foothills Publishing published her first chapbook,* Water Pistol Suicide Pose, *in November of last year. Her work has been featured in* Poem of the Day, The Red Bridge Review, Ygdrasil, Write-Away-Poetry, *and* Subtle Tea.

ANITA DARCEL TAYLOR
on writing *A Slight Case of Hypomania*

I don't recall the force behind the urgency to write *A Slight Case of Hypo-mania*. In retrospect, I realize that I was hypomanic when the first draft plopped itself onto the page and was fighting the need to submit again to medications, to the lethargy and dullness that treatment had brought in the past. How to strike a balance? I was and remain disturbed by the notion of drug as panacea, drug as the ticket to normality, and find false the rhetoric presented in television commercials by pharmaceutical companies; take a pill and you'll be social, happy, and carefree. I needed to explore my experience on and off drugs, weigh the consequences of each. I was a bit surprised to see that chief among my concerns was the impact, if any, of drug therapy on my ability to write. I feared that if I didn't find some sort of reconciliation between drug therapy and an active and curious mind, I would forgo med-ications completely. I'm not convinced that I found answers, although, this work gave language to the questions. I think that only through living will the answers reveal themselves.

Anita Darcel Taylor, a native of Schenectady, NY, received a Master of Fine Arts degree from Bennington College. Excerpts from her upcoming collection of interconnected personal essays have been published in the Potomac Literary Review *and anthologies entitled* The Use of Personal Narratives in the Help-ing Professions *and* Under Her Skin: How Girls Experience Race in America. *Currently, she lives in Washington, DC.*

TRUTH THOMAS on writing *Naptural*

I lived in London once and saw a sea of African descent people in dred locs, intricate cornrows, and very few perms. Burdened with African American cultural baggage, I found it odd. After two years living near Brixton, I picked up a copy of *Ebony* magazine, saw all the ads aimed at "relaxing" our hair to mirror Europeans and realized the oddity was us.

Truth Thomas is a musician and poet from Washington, D.C. Musically, Thomas incorporates a wide range of musical expression from the African Diaspora and beyond to form his own personal artistic expression. In his poetry, he strives to marry the crafts of "page and stage" in an introspective.

SOME OF MY ALL-TIME FAVORITES...

NONNIE AUGUSTINE

Poets who have been a strong influence on me include Raymond Carver, Emily Dickenson and Wallace Stevens. There is a book edited by Garrison Keillor called *Good Poems,* in which, every poem is a gem. At the moment, my favorite poem is one by James Wright, "A Blessing," which leaves me breathless every time I read it. And Richard Rhodes' book, *How to Write,* is, in my opinion, brilliant.

CATHLEEN RICHARDSON BAILEY

My favorite books begin in childhood. Beverly Cleary's *Ellen Tibbits,* a story of friendship, insecurity and woolen underwear. In high school, I devoured *A Tale of Two Cities, Rebecca* and *Lorna Doone.* As a young adult, my reading appetite yearned for people and stories like me. Enter Alice Walker's *The Color Purple,* Toni Morrison's *Song of Solomon* and Zora Neale Hurston's *Their Eyes Were Watching God.* They are wonderfully written stories about how to do and not do life. Arna Bontemps and Langston Hughes co-authored a delightful book titled *Popo and Fifina.* The language is rich and sets you right down there on the island. Other books include Eleanora Tate's *The Minstrel's Melody,* Tupac Shakur's *The Rose That Grew From Concrete,* and all the Harry Potter books. Each of these authors understands what I call "noble requirements"—sense of character, language (words, rhythm, and texture) and then story, in that order. I like it when stories take me away, prevent me from putting the book down, and inspire me to write.

MARK BUDMAN

One of my favorite books of all time is *Master and Margarita* by Mikhail Bulgakov. This short novel has everything that my heart desires. I love its intensity, its flight of fantasy, its unabridged sensuality, its wry humor, its memorable characters and unforgettable plot. *Master and Margarita* is deeply rooted in the Russian culture and yet it delves into history, religion, and magic at the same time.

RICK CASTANEDA

One of my favorite books is Raymond Carver's *Where I'm Calling From: Selected Stories,* because about three-fourths of the way through one of his stories, I'm always thinking how simple it is, and how I could easily write such a story. And then the end of the story whips around, and I realize I can never come close. It's not that his stories have surprise endings; it's just that they're so...truthful.

PATRICIA GOMES

Let's go with *Jane Eyre* by Charlotte Bronte. Why? What more could one possibly ask of a story?! Rejection, isolation, madness, romance, and murder wrapped up in subtle feminism.

The Stand by Stephen King. Nearly the entire world wiped out in mere weeks by the nastiest of all viruses ever whipped up in a government testing lab. (A writer's dream, by the way: absolute quiet, no deadlines, no other commitments...freedom to write unencumbered by daily obligations.) All who remain must choose to stand on the side of good or evil for a final confrontation. The characters in this tome are so well-defined that they've taken on lives of their own. Long after you've closed the covers, and at the oddest of moments, you'll find yourself wondering how Fran and Stu are doing. And what's Tom Cullen collecting now? *The Stand* is King's masterpiece.

Anything by Truman Capote. Any book, any story, any barbed-wire interview. Never at a loss for words, Capote was a literary craftsman!

NOAH GROSSMAN

A favorite poem of mine is A.R. Ammons's "Stand-In." Elegant, funny, a good story, and best of all, it's observational poetry.

DEBBIE ANN ICE

I think the most brilliant book I have ever read has to be *The Sound and The Fury* by William Faulkner. His ability to step inside the heads of characters and show complex family relationships struggling with a confused society is amazing. The story is one of those that is so well-crafted, so brilliant, its meaning and importance transcend time.

A more contemporary book I truly love is *Housekeeping* by Marilynne Robinson—another disturbing family. The character Ruth steps off the page and sits down with you as you read. This writing is so insightful, so brilliant. It's a book you read slowly, pausing to linger on a word, a phrase, a thought. Oh, and I love collections, my favorite being Alice Munro's *Hateship, Friendship...* She is the queen of the short story, the master of lyrical prose.

DAN JAFFE

Some of my all-time favorite books are Tolstoy's *Anna Karenina* and Flaubert's *Madame Bovary* for their social daring and mastery of technique, Dostoevsky's *Crime and Punishment* for its psychological depth and narrative voice, Gogol's *Dead Souls* for its hilarious wit, Toni Morrison's *Beloved* for its gut-wrenching power, and Dorothy Allison's *Bastard Out of Carolina* for the power of its rhythmic prose.

PAMELA MACISAAC

These are my favorite books—or the top 10 anyway—in random order:

Vanity Fair by William Thackeray
The Catcher in the Rye by J.D. Salinger
Emily of New Moon (and many other books) by Lucy Maude Montgomery
Any collection of stories by Mavis Gallant
Middlemarch by George Eliot
The Group by Mary McCarthy
The Lives of Girls and Women by Alice Munro
Beautiful Joe by Margaret Marshall Saunders
The Pursuit of Love/Love in a Cold Climate by Nancy Mitford
All of the Rabbit Angstrom books by John Updike

I'm sure that I'll think of others with a slap to the head in the next week or so!

MARCIA LYNX QUALEY

Three of my all-time favorites are Dostoevsky, *The Idiot;* Naguib Mahfouz, *Cairo Trilogy;* and Halldor Laxness, *Independent People.* I like giant books that contain whole worlds and eras, with strong, flawed characters. Twentieth century Egypt is gone, but with a copy of the *Cairo Trilogy,* you could continue to live inside it and know it. The same goes for pre-World War II Iceland. When I love a book, I have to move in with the author. Fyodor made me move to Russia. Halldor made me visit Iceland, but it was a bit too cold to stay. Naguib really made up my mind.

SHANNON QUINN

Some of my favorite books are *A Complicated Kindness,* by Miriam Toews, *A Prayer for Owen Meaney,* by John Irving and *The House of Leaves,* by Mark Z. Danielewski. For me, these books were all about feeling a fierce relationship with the characters.

HALIMAT SEKULA

I love Charles Dickens for his ability to find humor in human frailty. I like his book *Hard Times* best, I think. Alice Walker, the day I finished reading *The Color Purple,* I kept saying "Thank you, thank you." I don't know why. I respect Ben Okri for *The Famished Road.* To me Okri is one of the finest post-colonial writers living.

JESS STUART

Alrighty then, here are a few my favorite books:

Jane Eyre by Charlotte Bronte. I read this when I was young (back when the earth was still cooling), and it was the first time I'd read a description of the death of a child. I remember thinking Helen couldn't really be dead, that she would reappear in the story and there would be some explanation about how Jane had only dreamt her death or some such. When the truth became clear to me, I felt as though someone had punched me in the stomach. I grieved for dear Helen for days afterward.

Wuthering Heights by Emily Bronte. I can only imagine the scandal this story caused when it first hit Victorian bookshelves. Lust, violence, obsession, and that scene where Heathcliff confesses to exhuming Catherine's body—yikes! It's a powerful story about the dark places to which love can sometimes take us.

And finally *The Bridges of Madison County* by Robert James Waller, because I'm a sucker for books that can make me cry.

KRISTI SWADLEY

Any book by Neil Gaiman is a favorite of mine, even if I haven't read it. He's that good. His comic book/Graphic Novel *Sandman* has been a huge influence on me. Gaiman proved to me that literature and art could meld seamlessly together and have a significant impact on both the literary and comic worlds.

On the poetry side, Charles Bukowski's *Love is a Dog From Hell* was the first book of poetry I ever bought, and it has had the greatest influence on my writing. Bukowski was the antithesis of the poetry I had read (and loathed) in school. The lack of bullshit was a breath of fresh air.

ANITA DARCEL TAYLOR

My life seems to unfold through a string of stages. *A Room of Her Own* marks a very young self who was questioning her identity and entitlement as woman, writer, and feminist. *The Price of the Ticket* became a sort of touchstone as I tried to give context to my experience of "otherness" within America and further, within the American black community. *The Golden Notebook* collided with apprehensions that boiled up in therapy shortly after I had been diagnosed manic-depressive. I was exhaustingly grateful to Andrew Solomon for his gift of *The Noonday Demon*. Before its publication, I could find no literary work that even acknowledged the significance of race, class, and culture on the manifestation and treatment of mental illness, let alone give space and exploration to those realities. And finally, the collected essays of Phillip Lopate (*Bachelorhood, Against Joie de Vivre,* and *Portrait of*

My Body) taught me, not only the value of self-exploration on the page, but also the literary beauty of the art form. If I was looking for permission to do what I do, Lopate gave me that permission.

TRUTH THOMAS

I love the work of E. Ethelbert Miller, and Tony Medina. While their voices are singular, both capture poetry powerfully, and frame it in activism. Whenever I think of writers who tirelessly work to nurture other black writers, I think of them.